This Book Belongs to

....

....

....

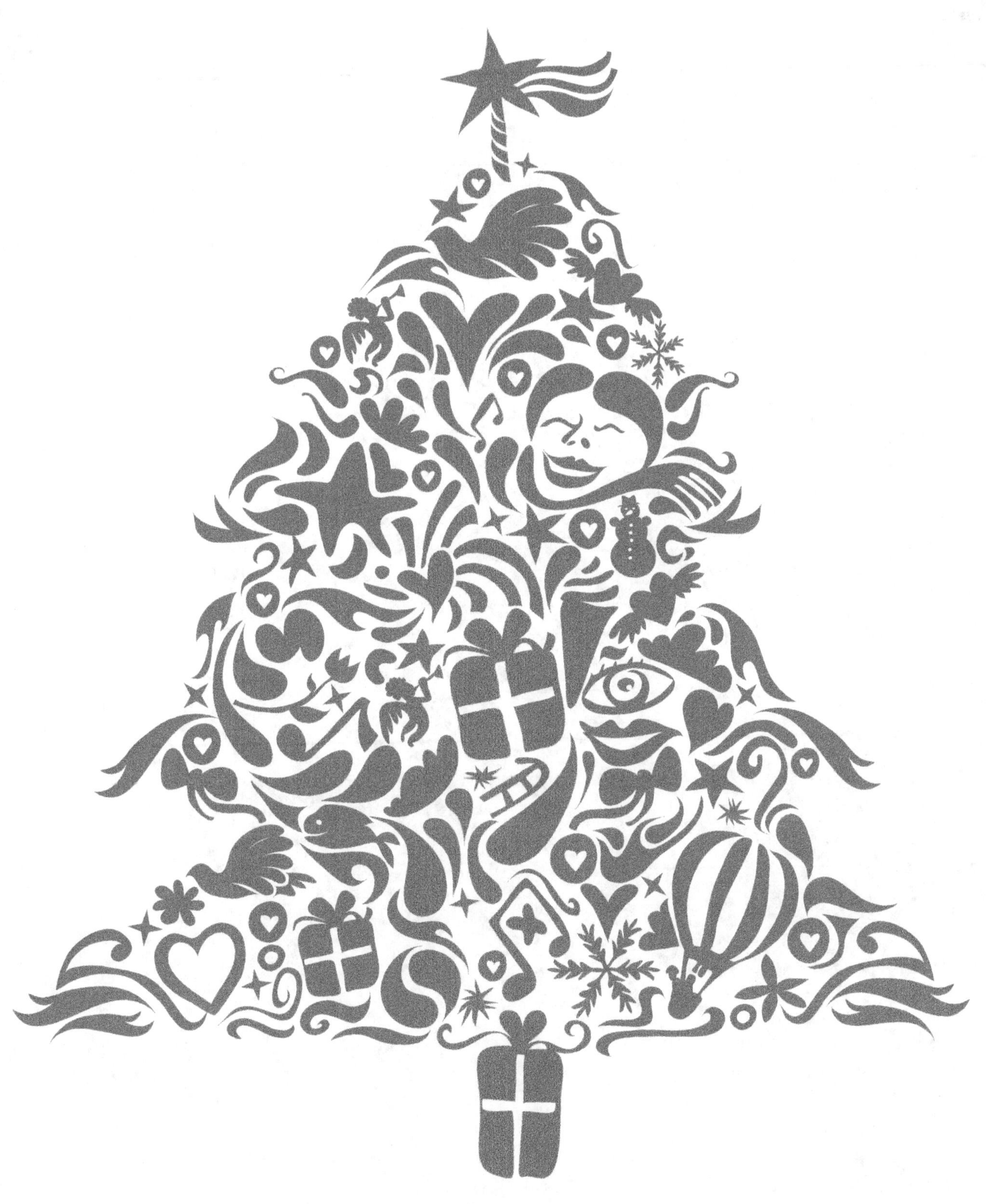

MERRY CHRISTMAS

Color Test

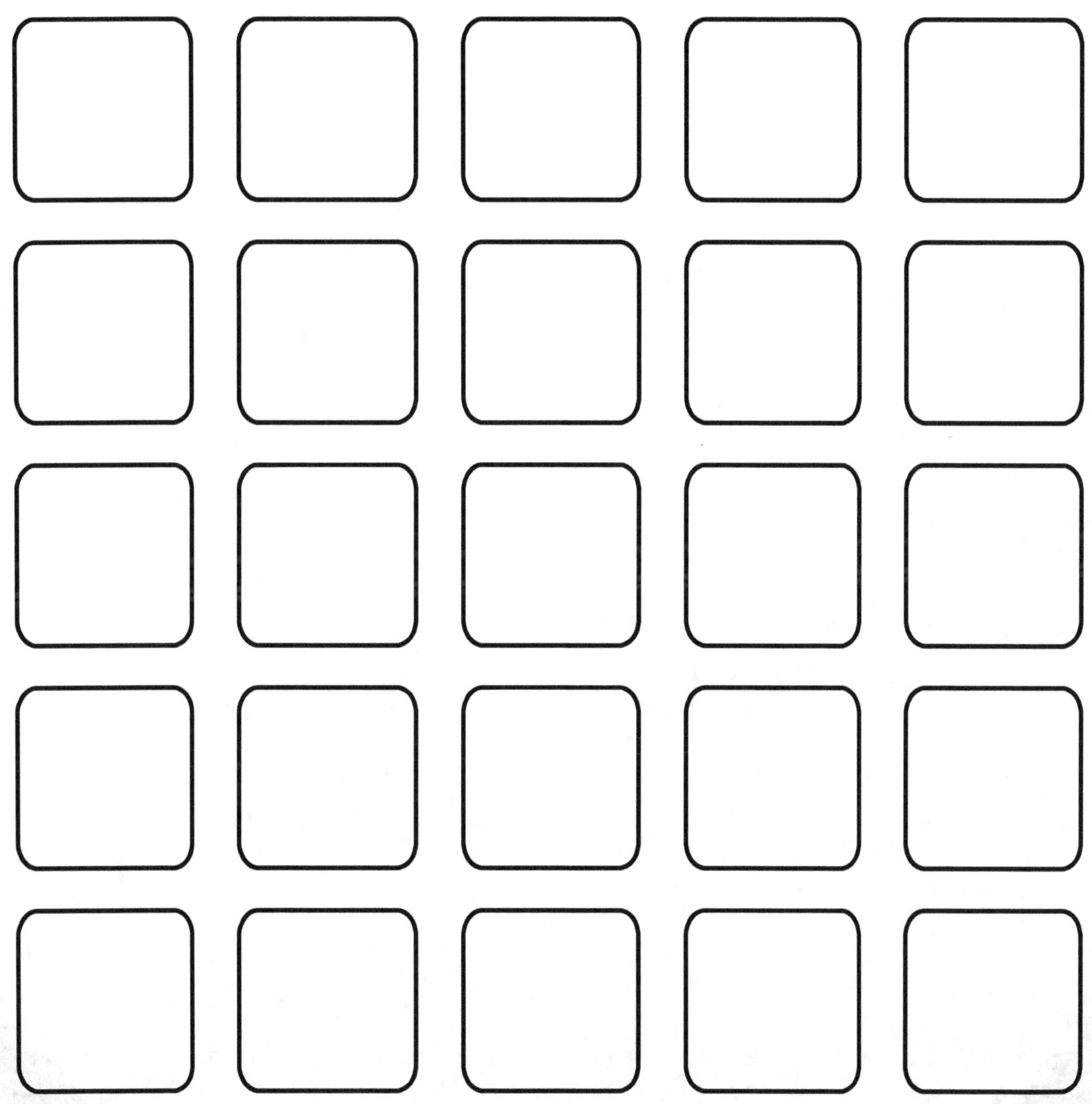

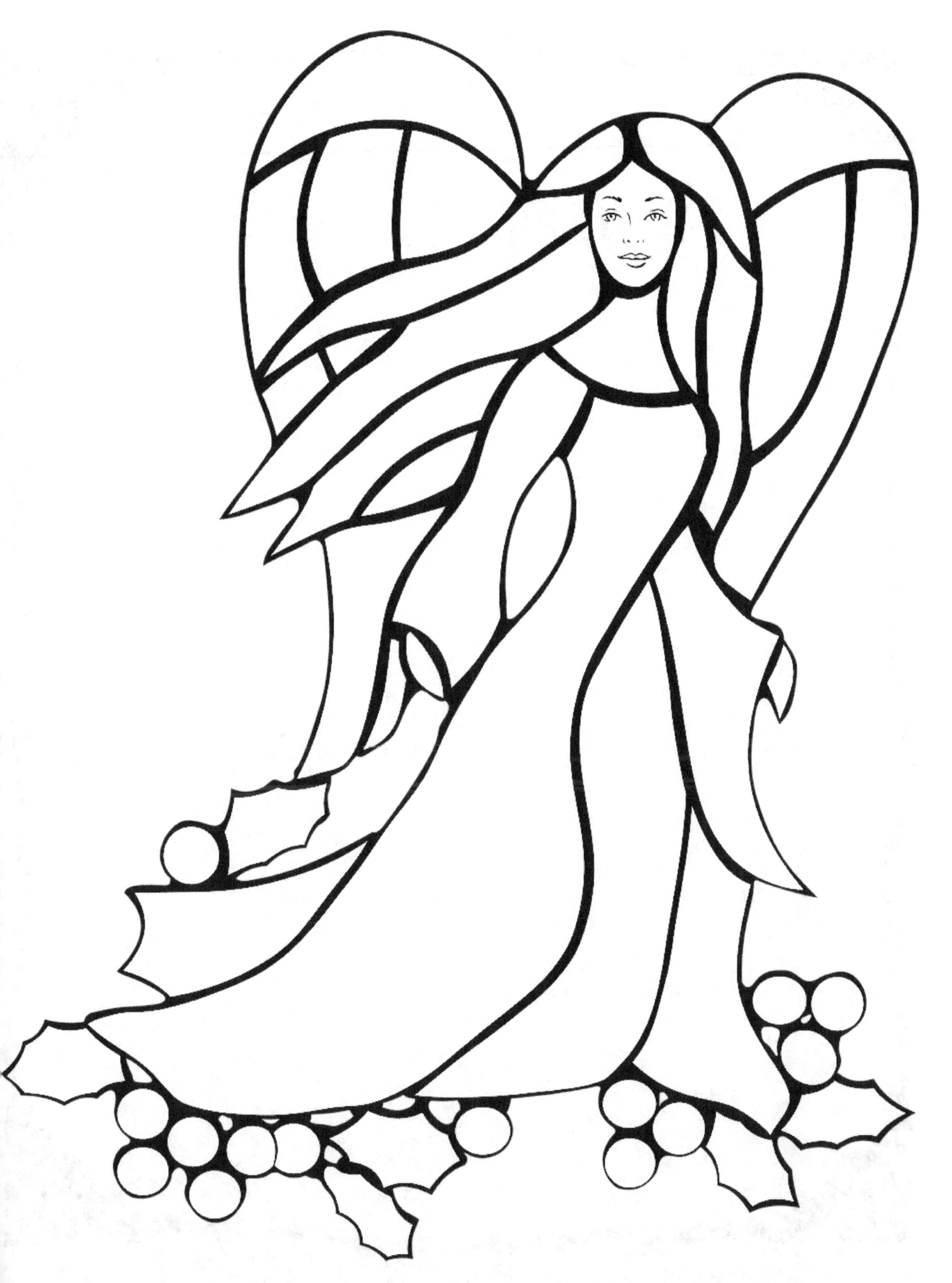

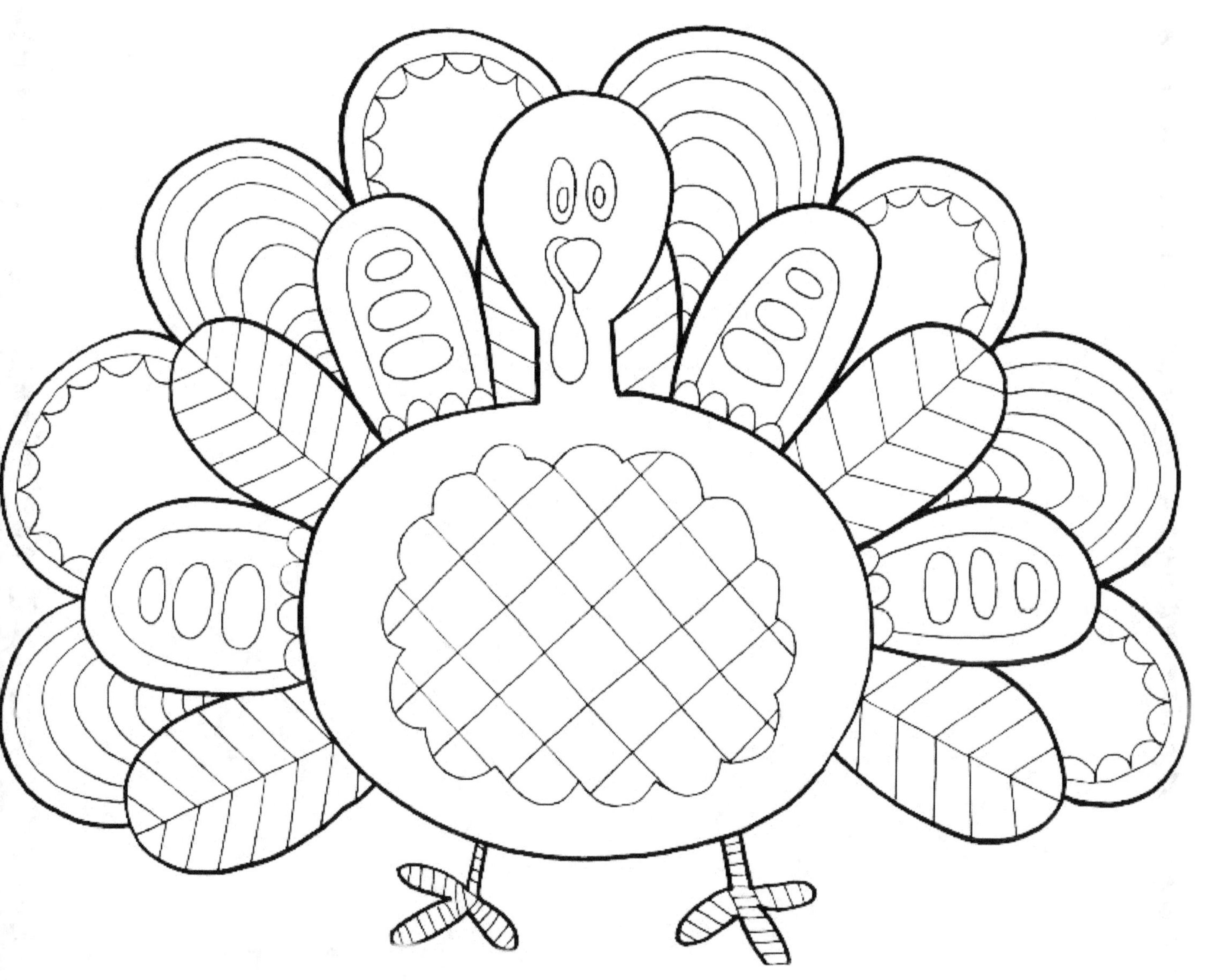

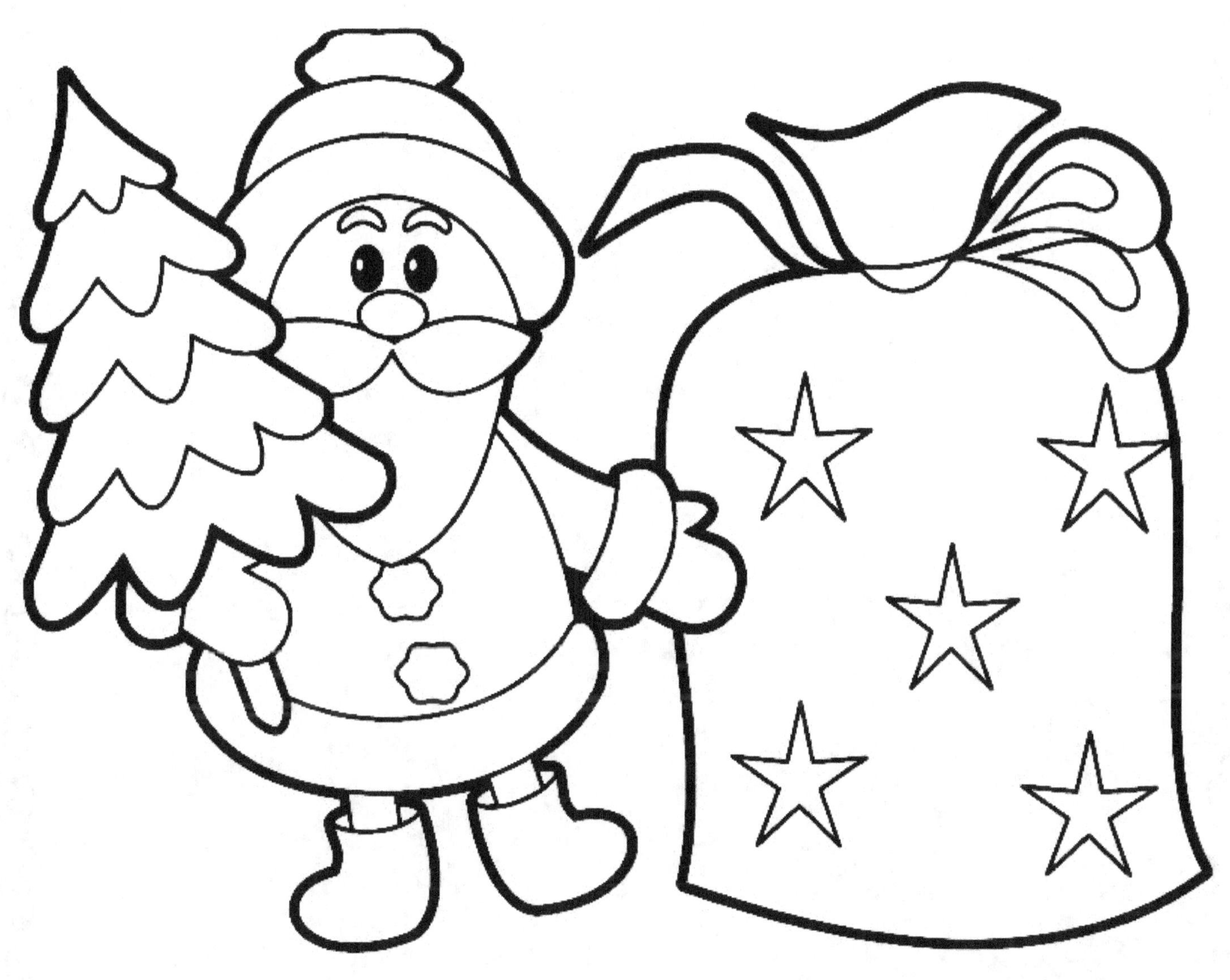

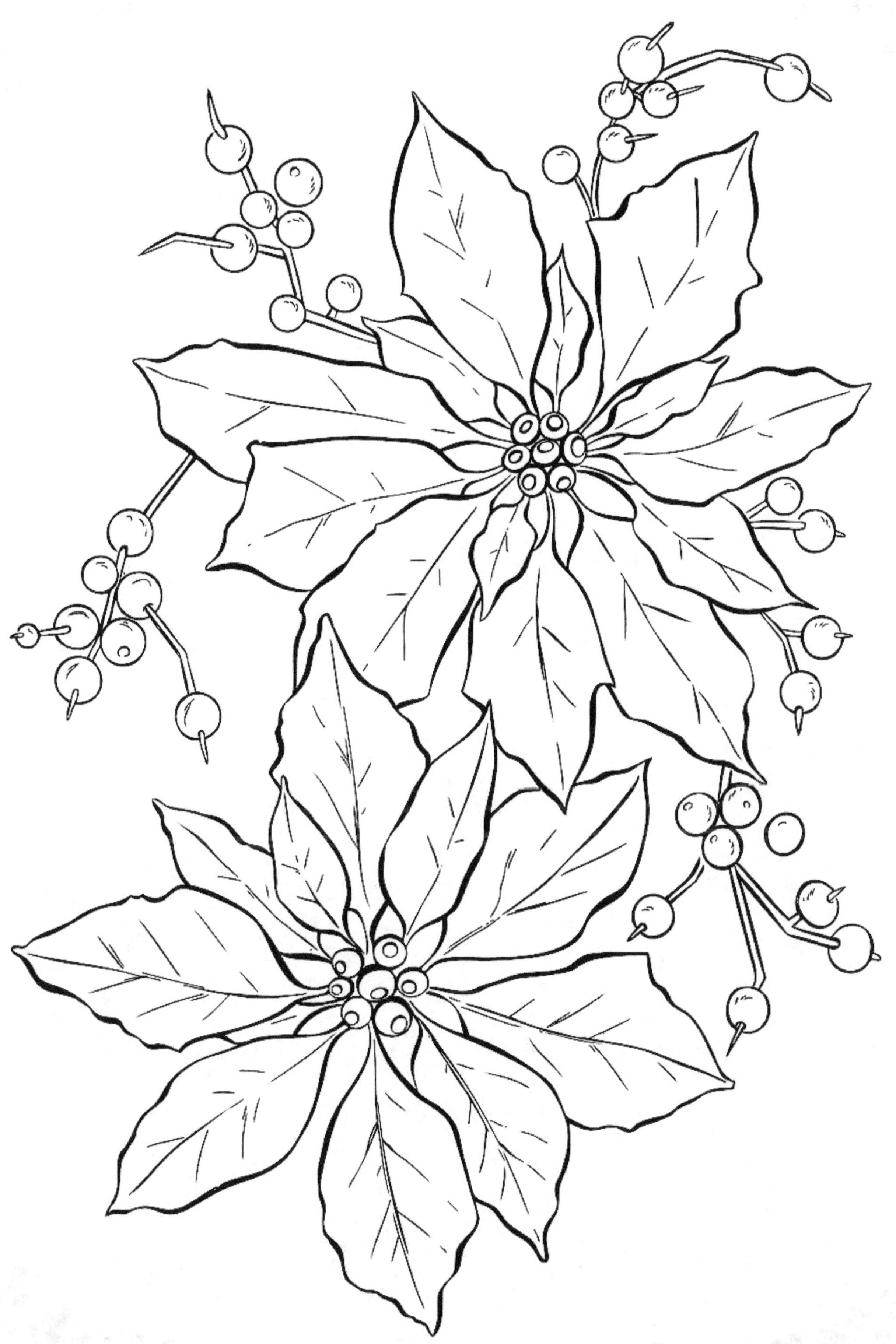

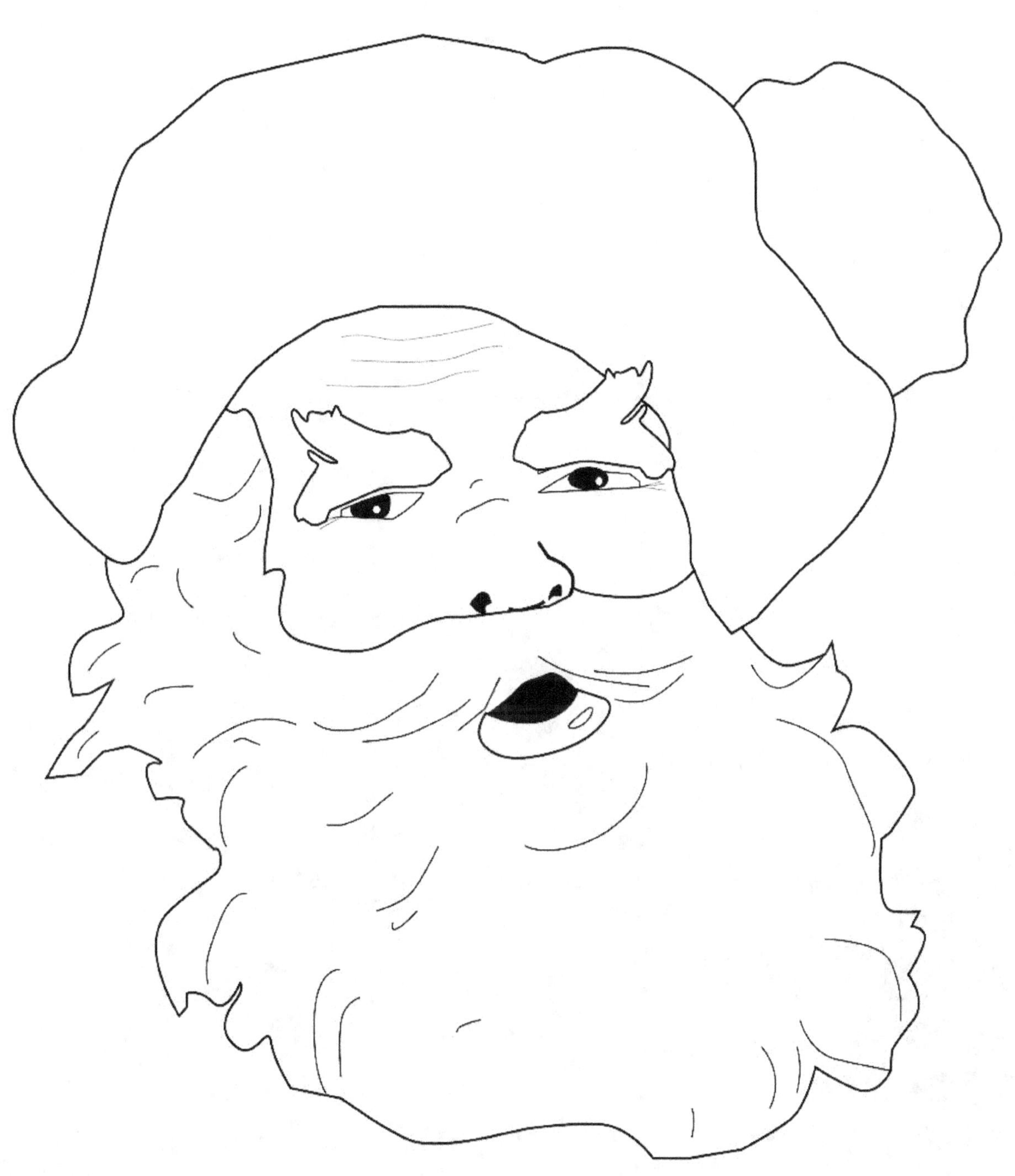

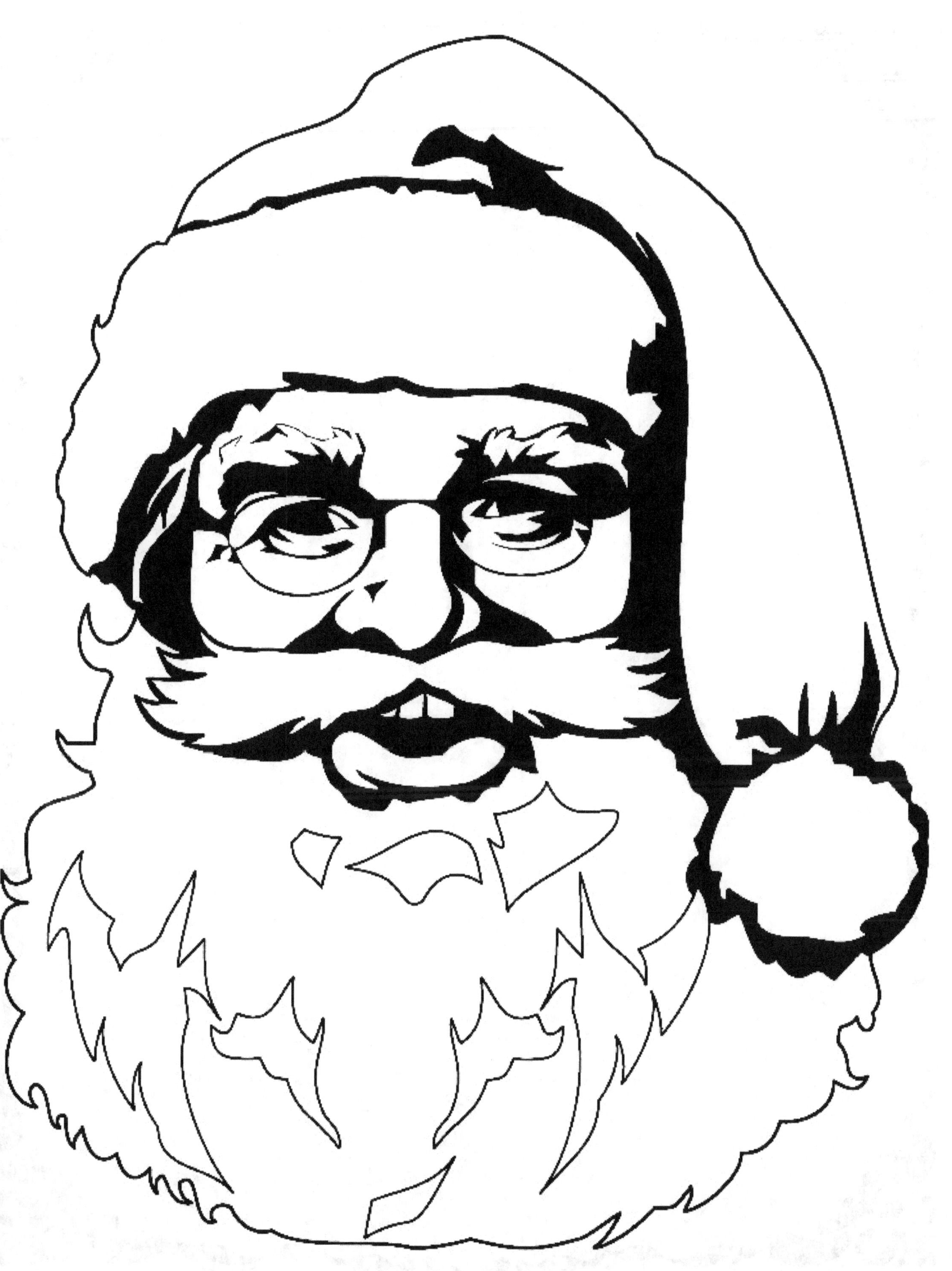

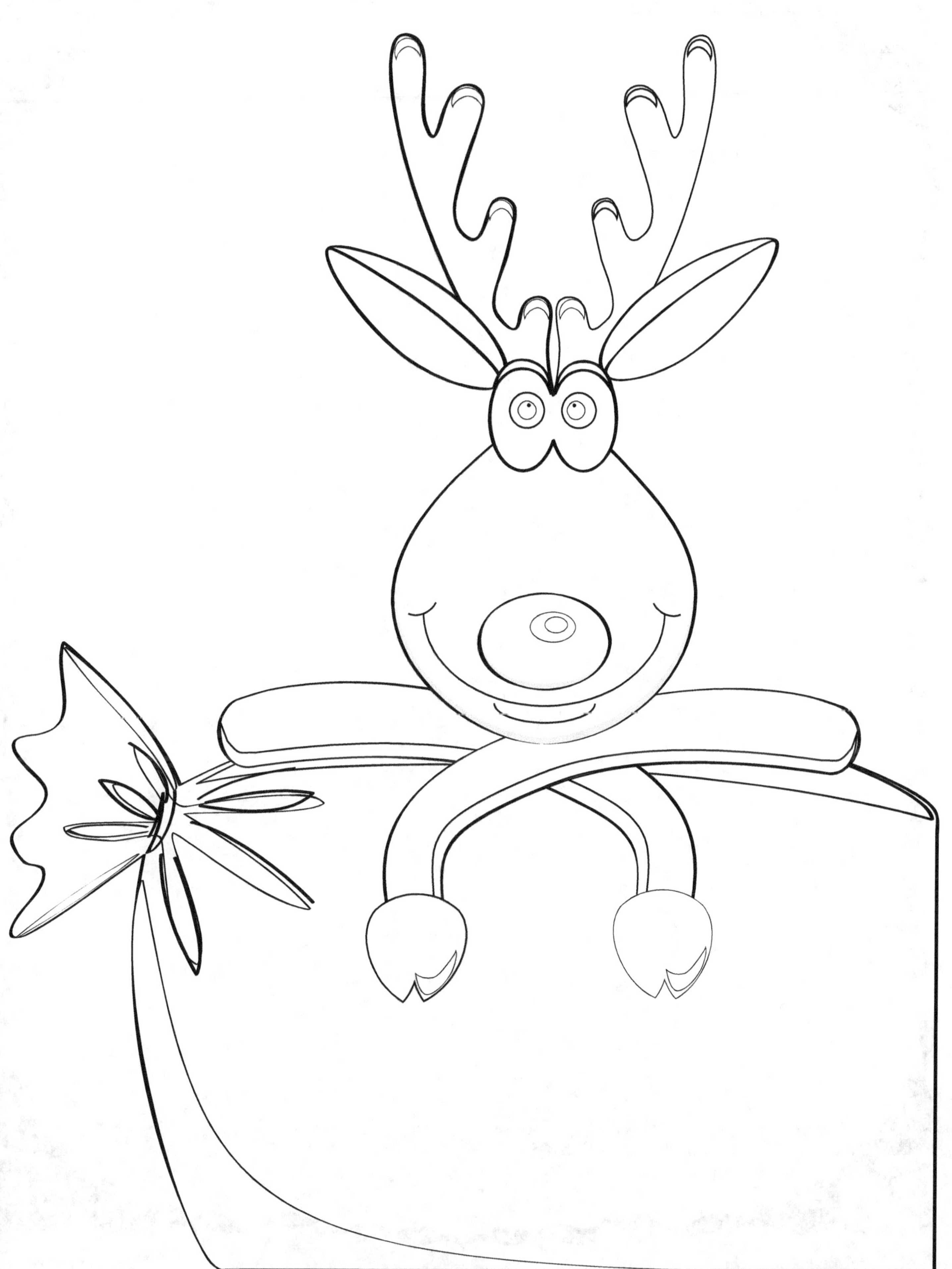

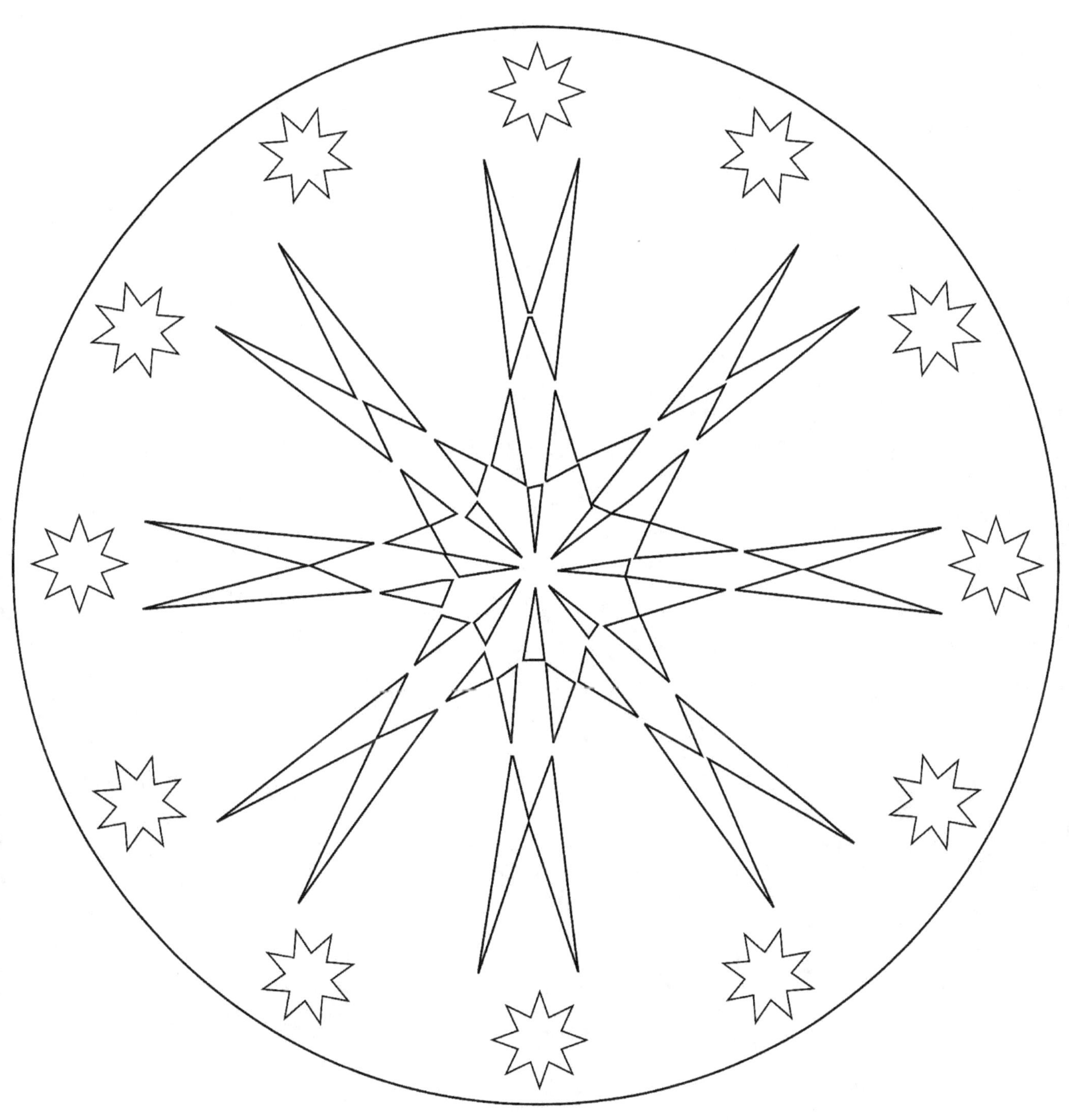

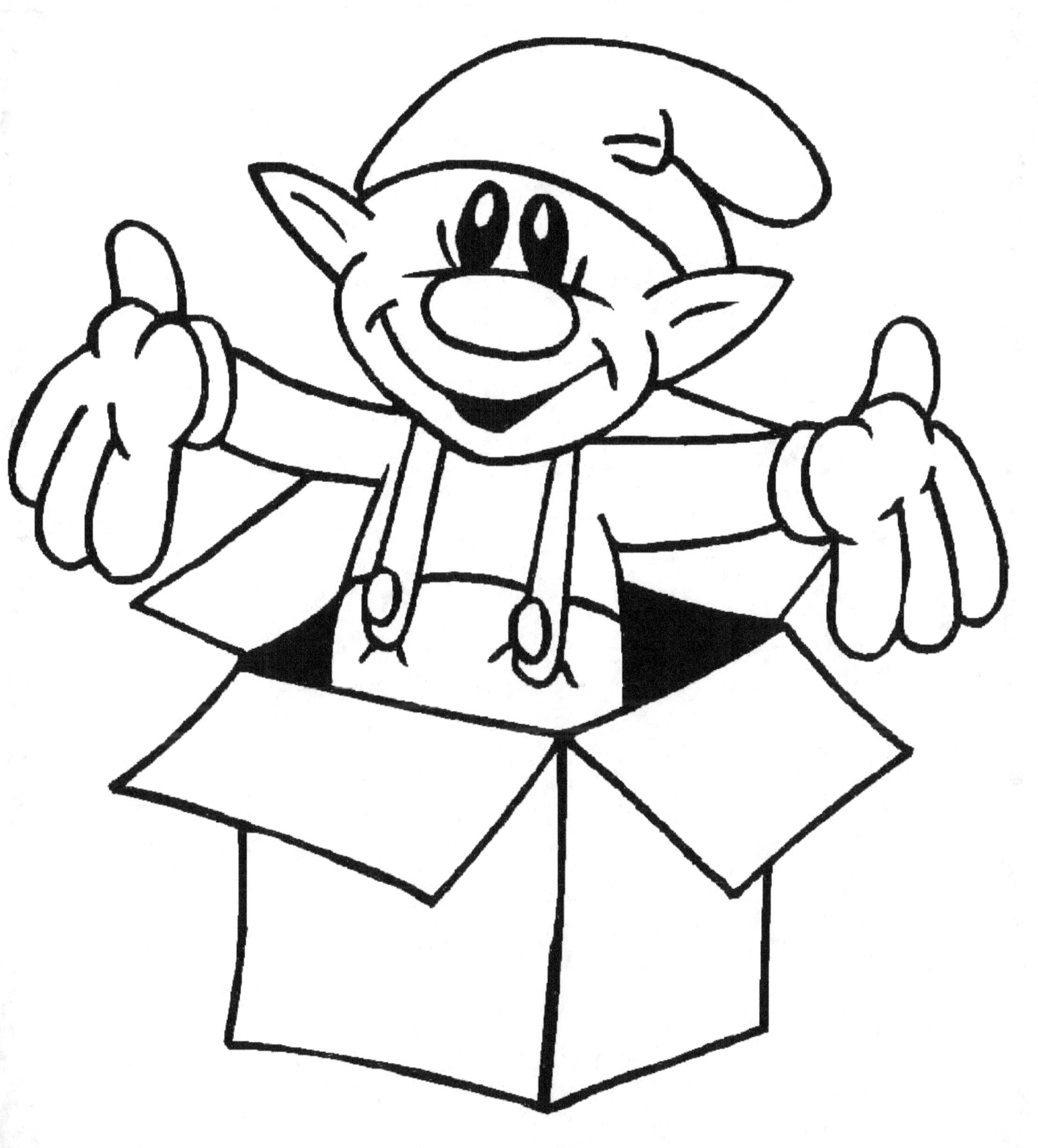

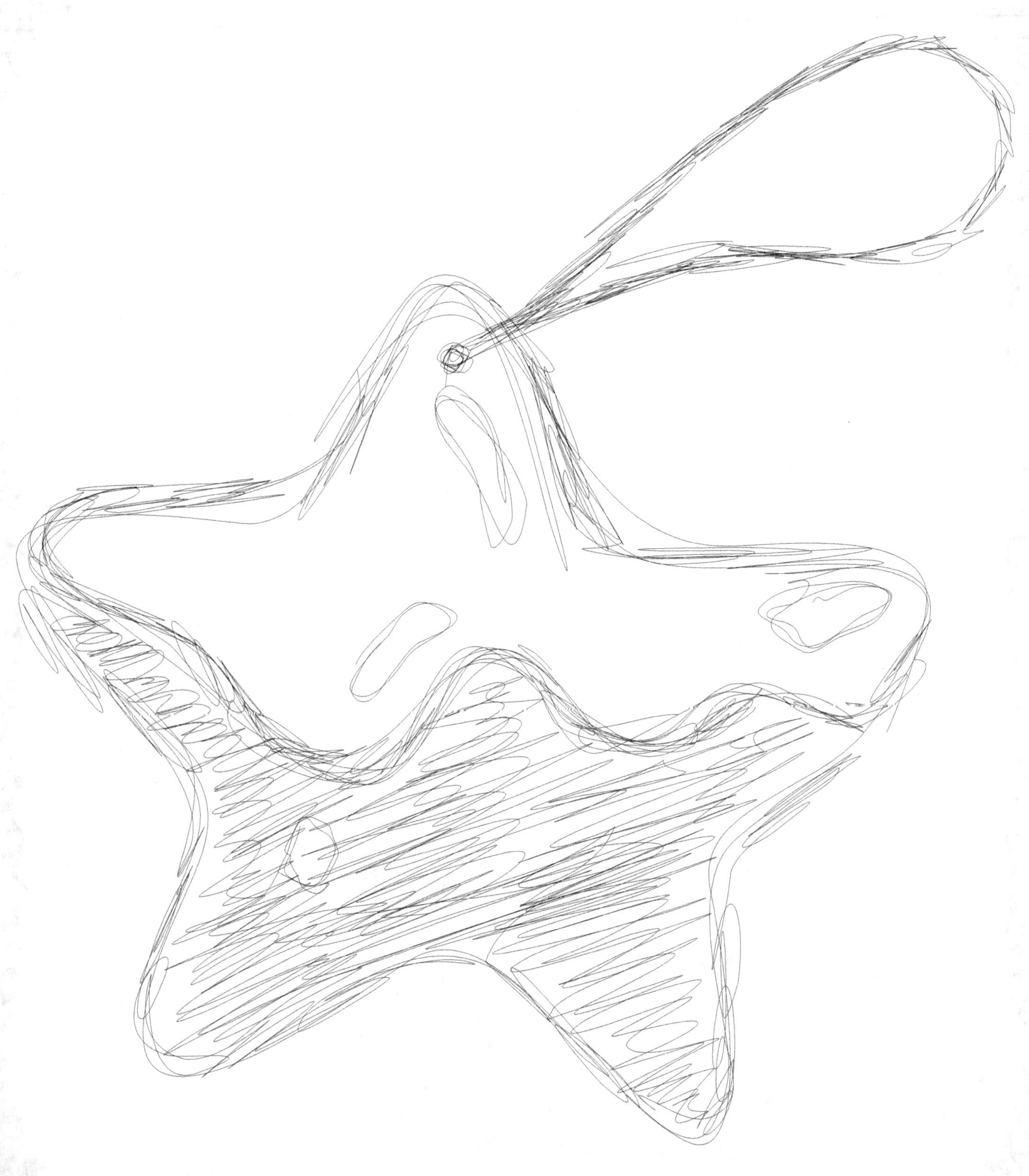

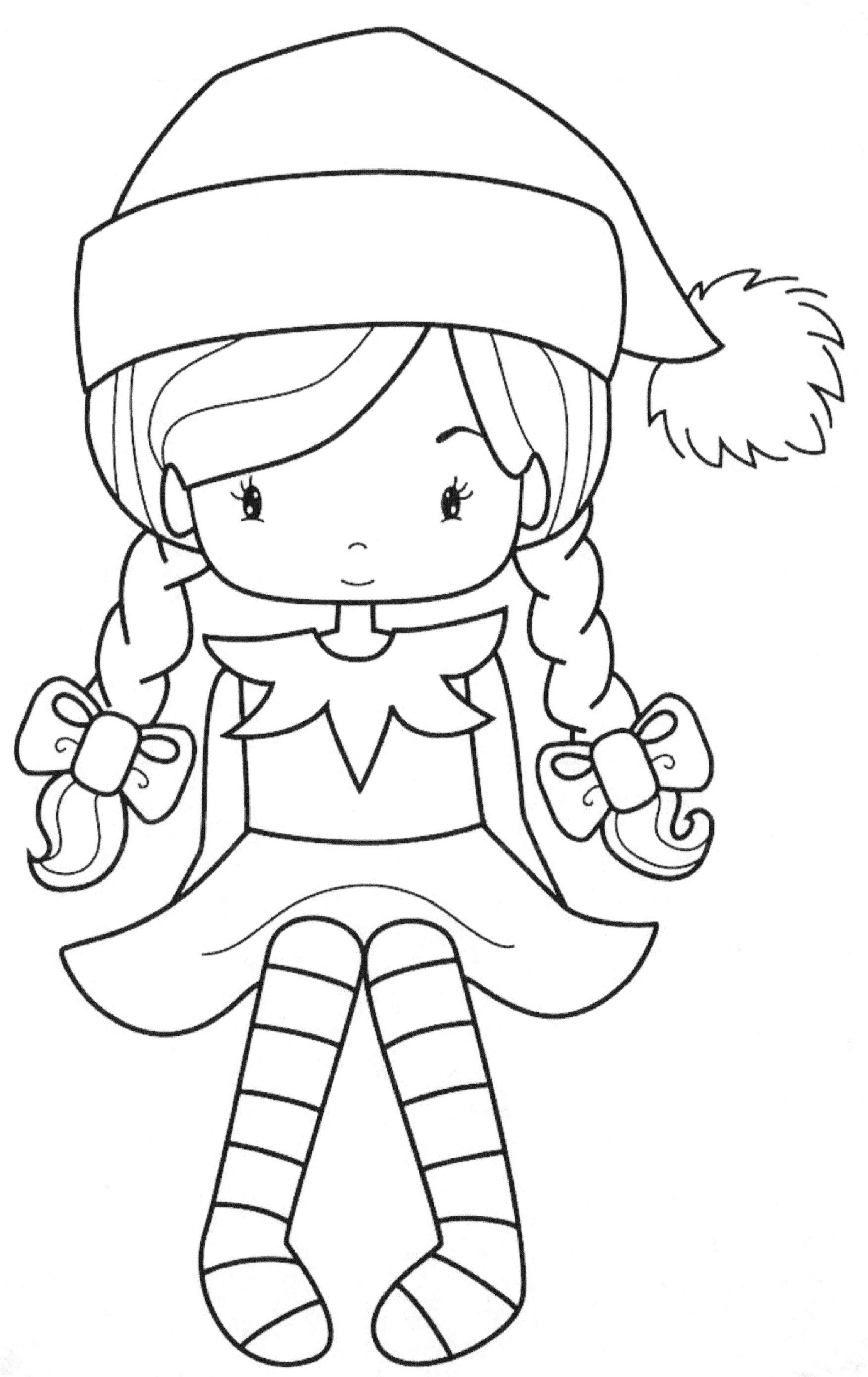

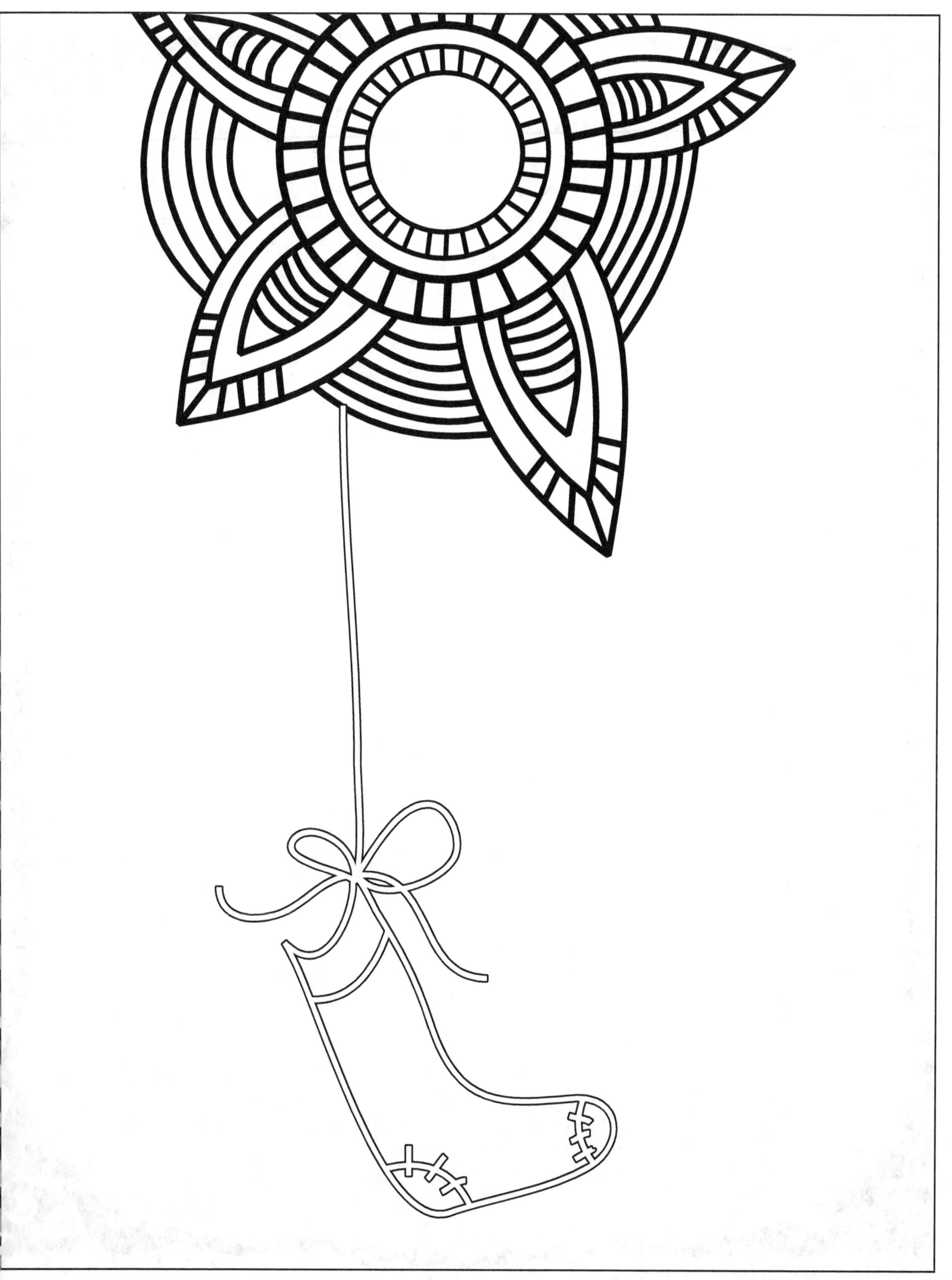

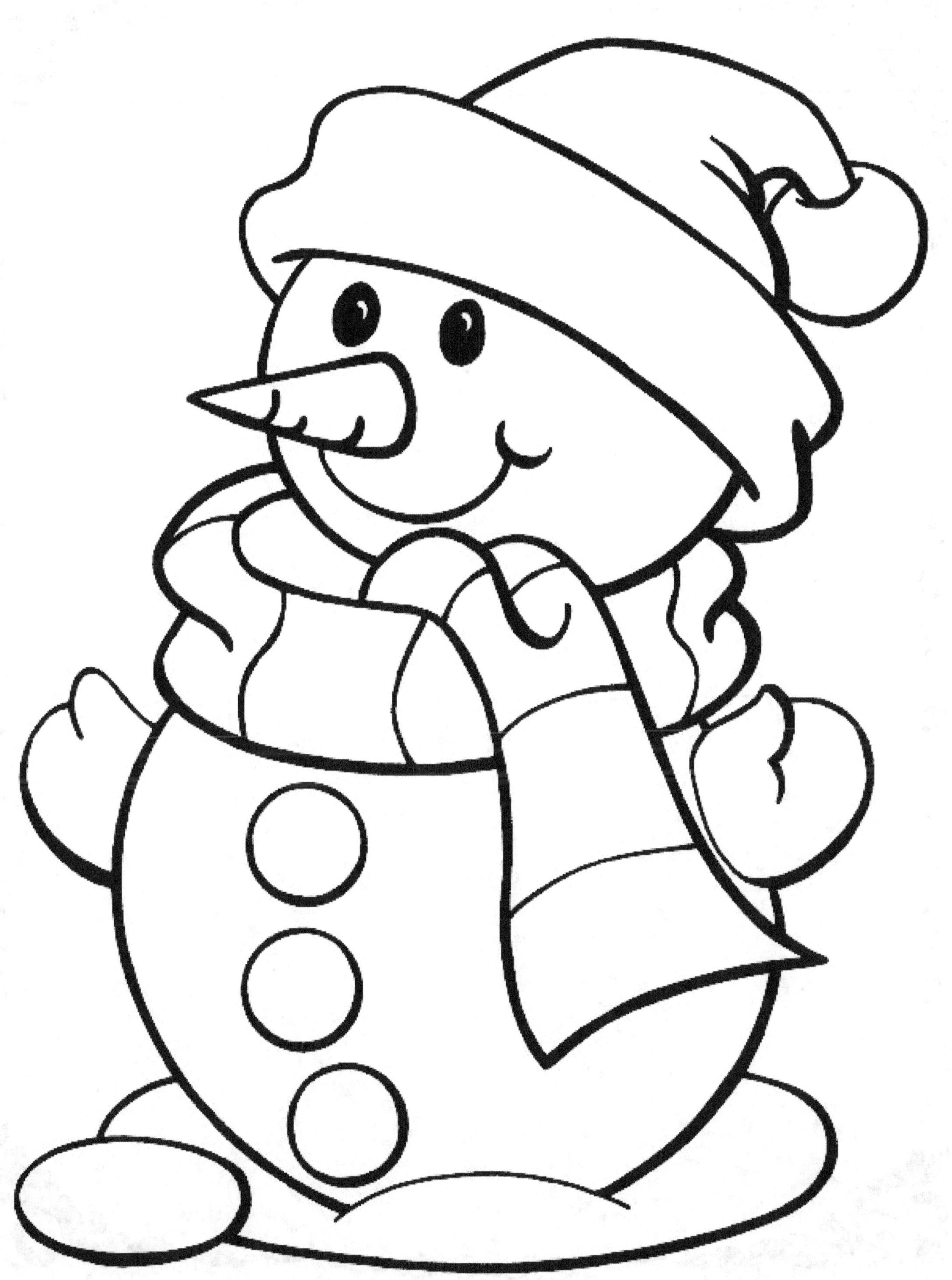

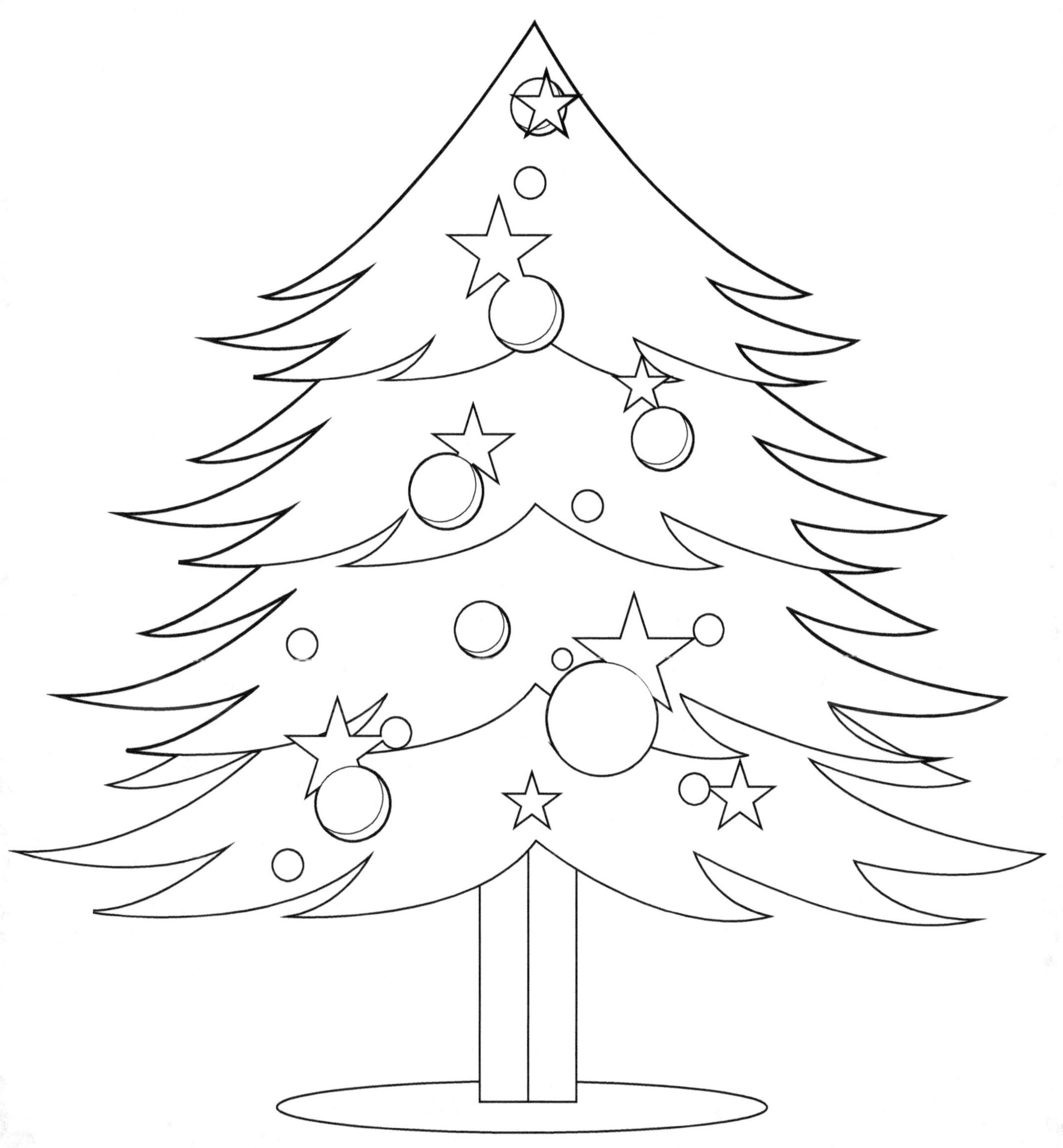

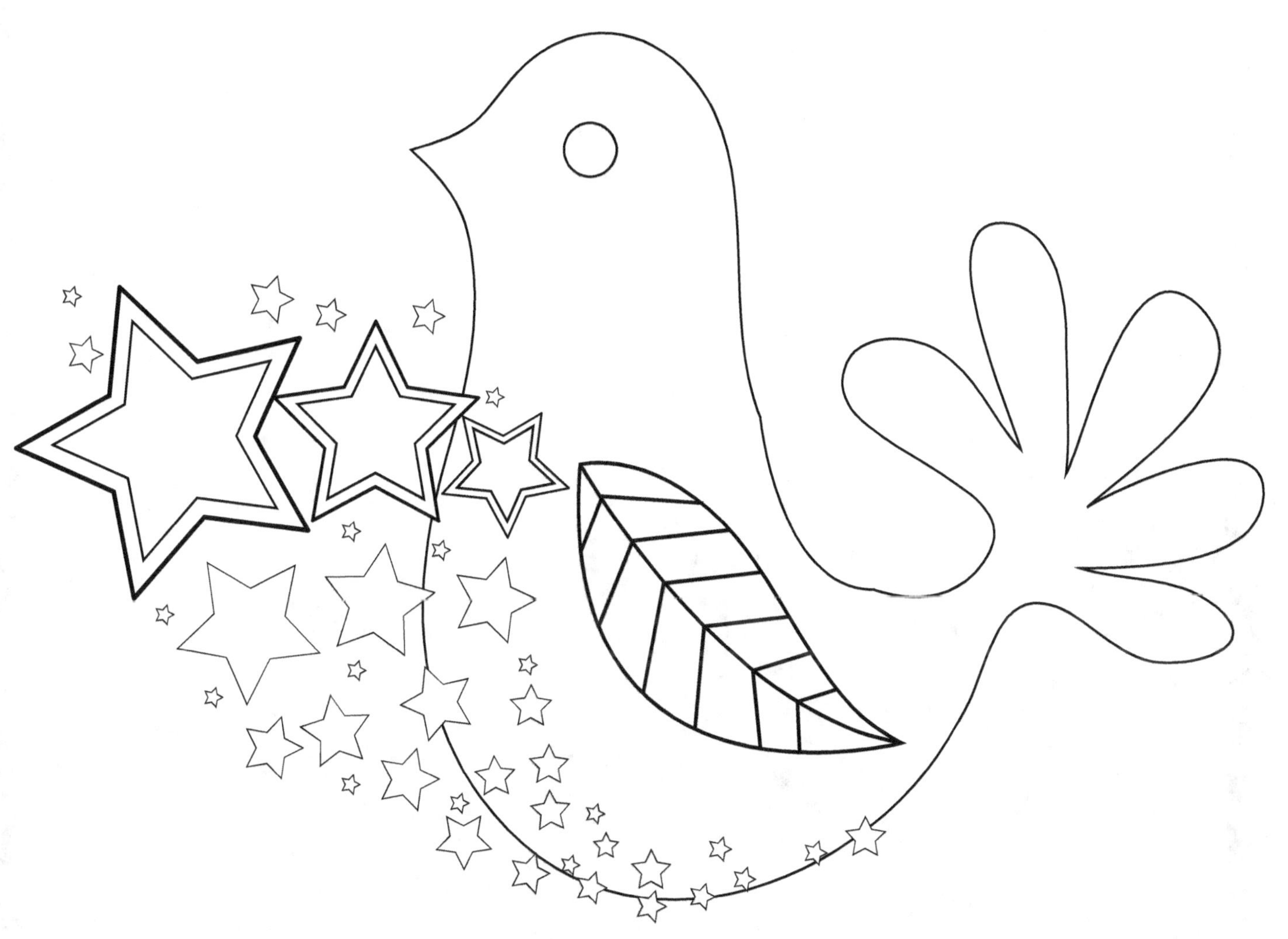

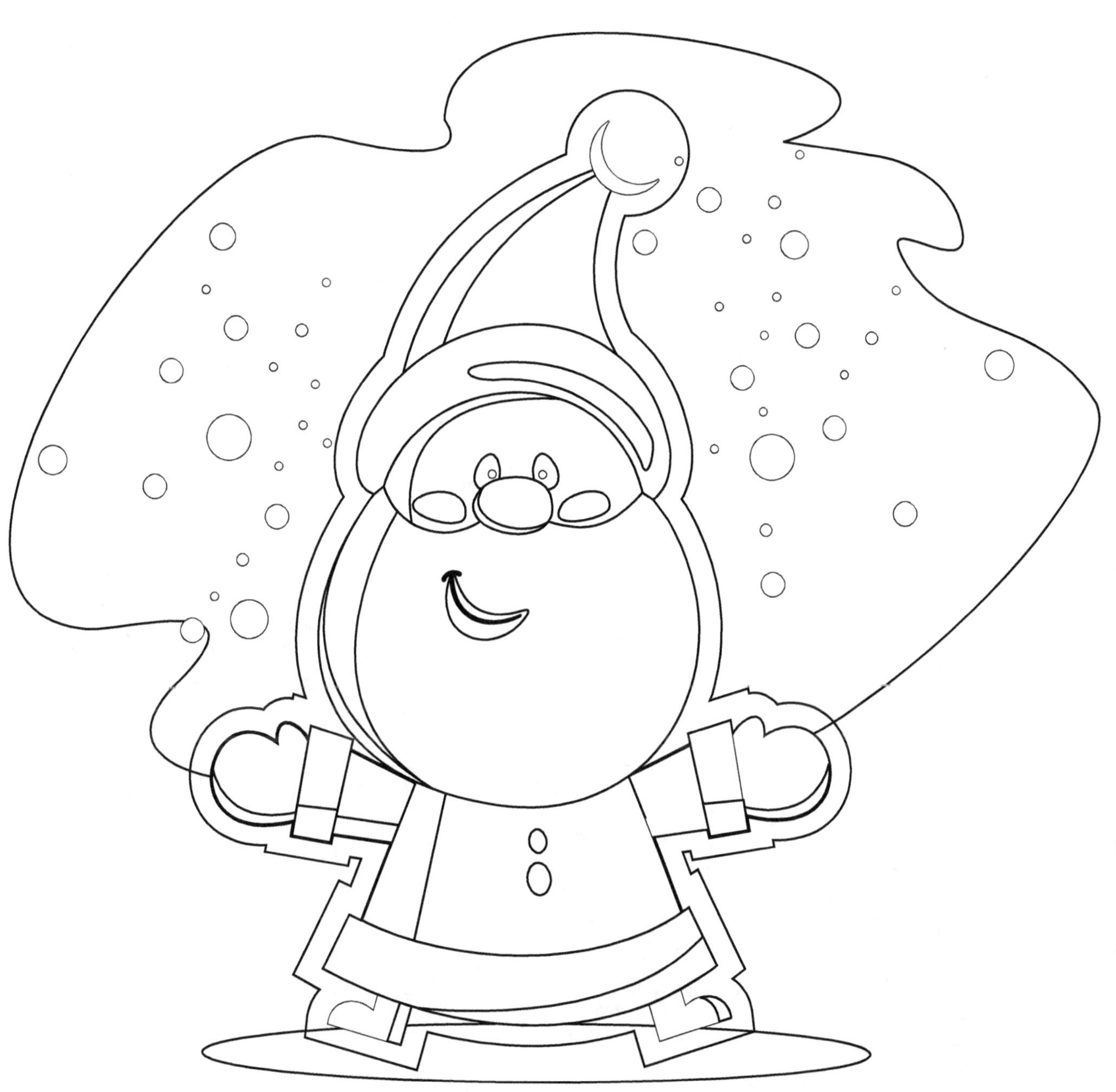

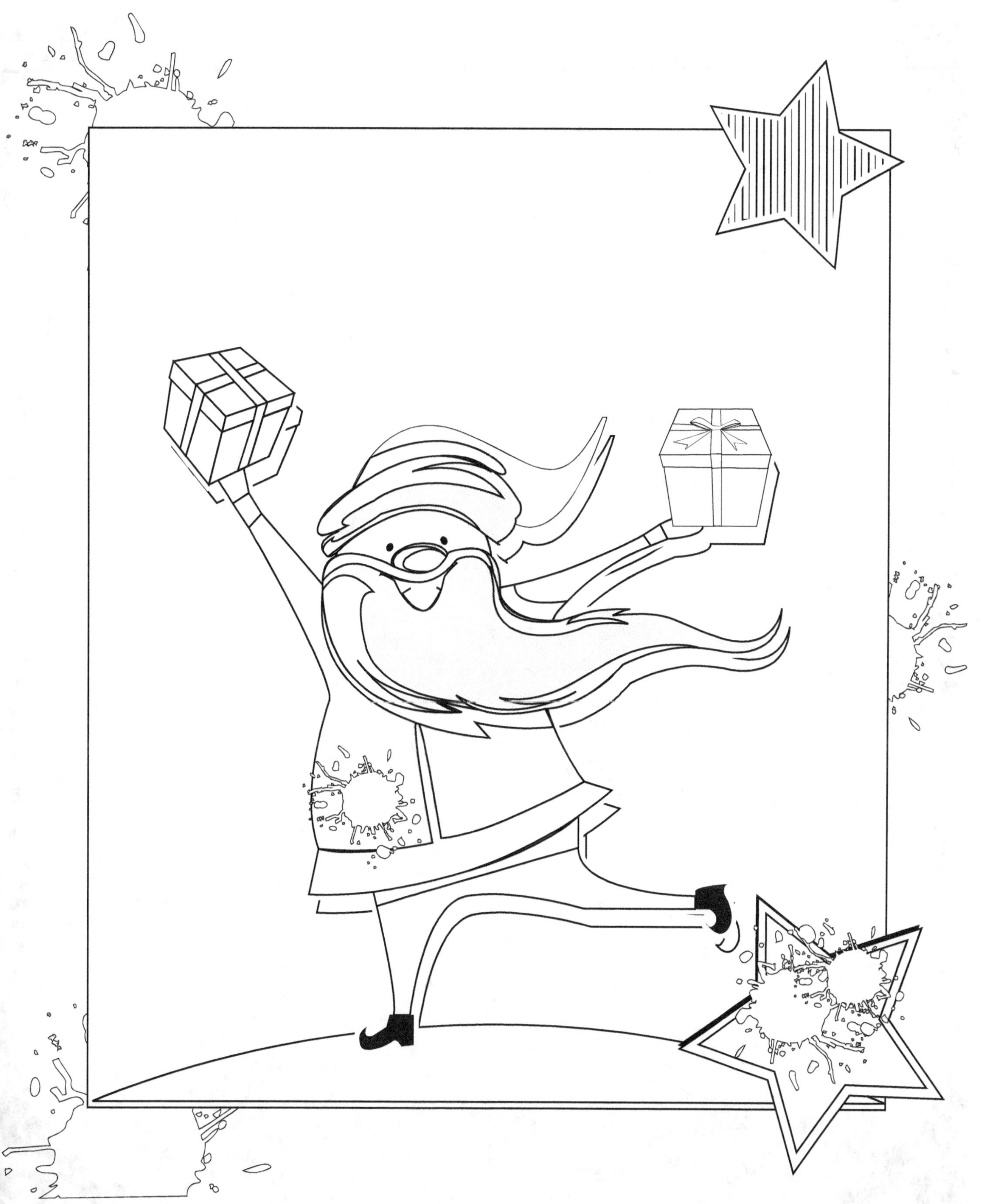

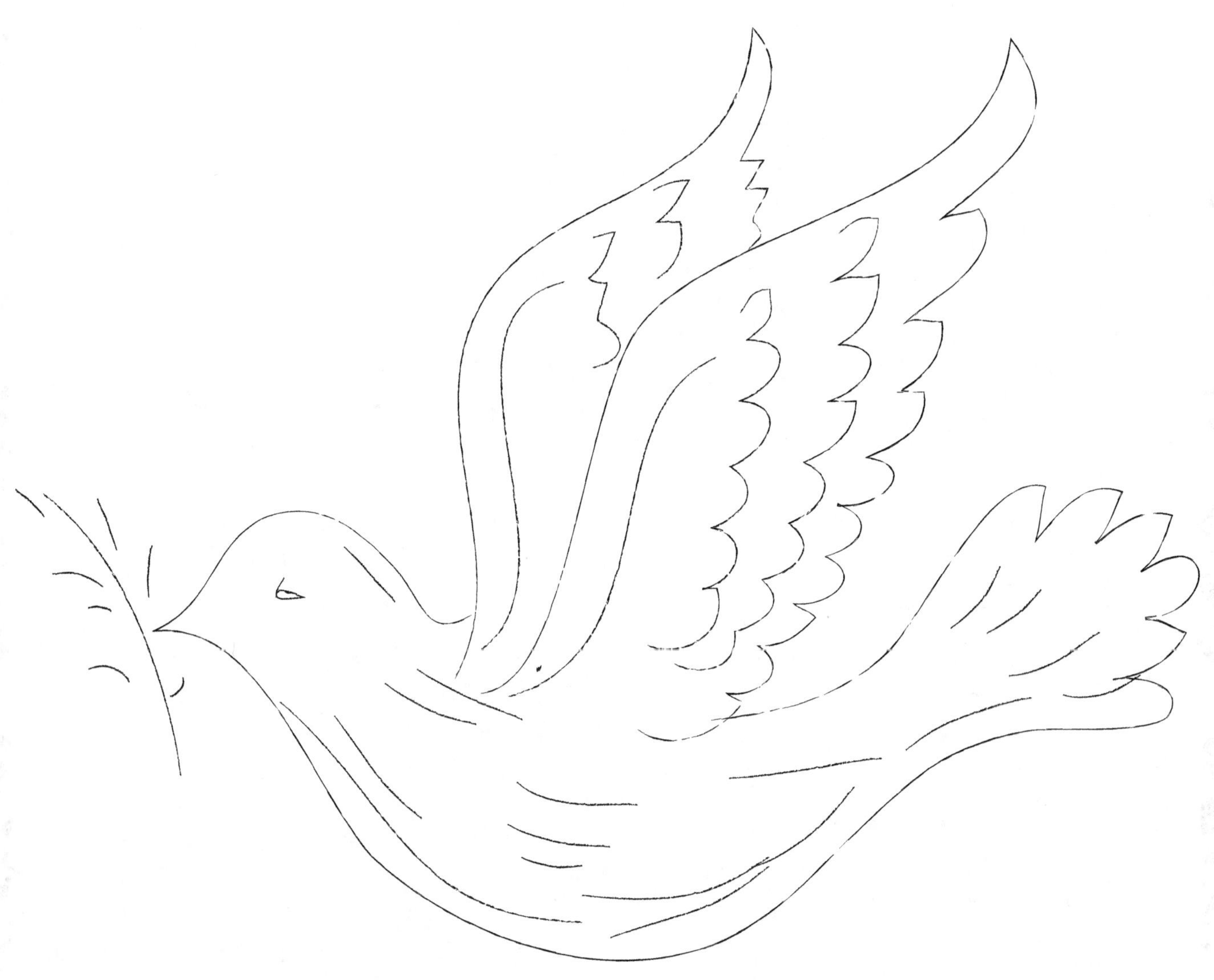

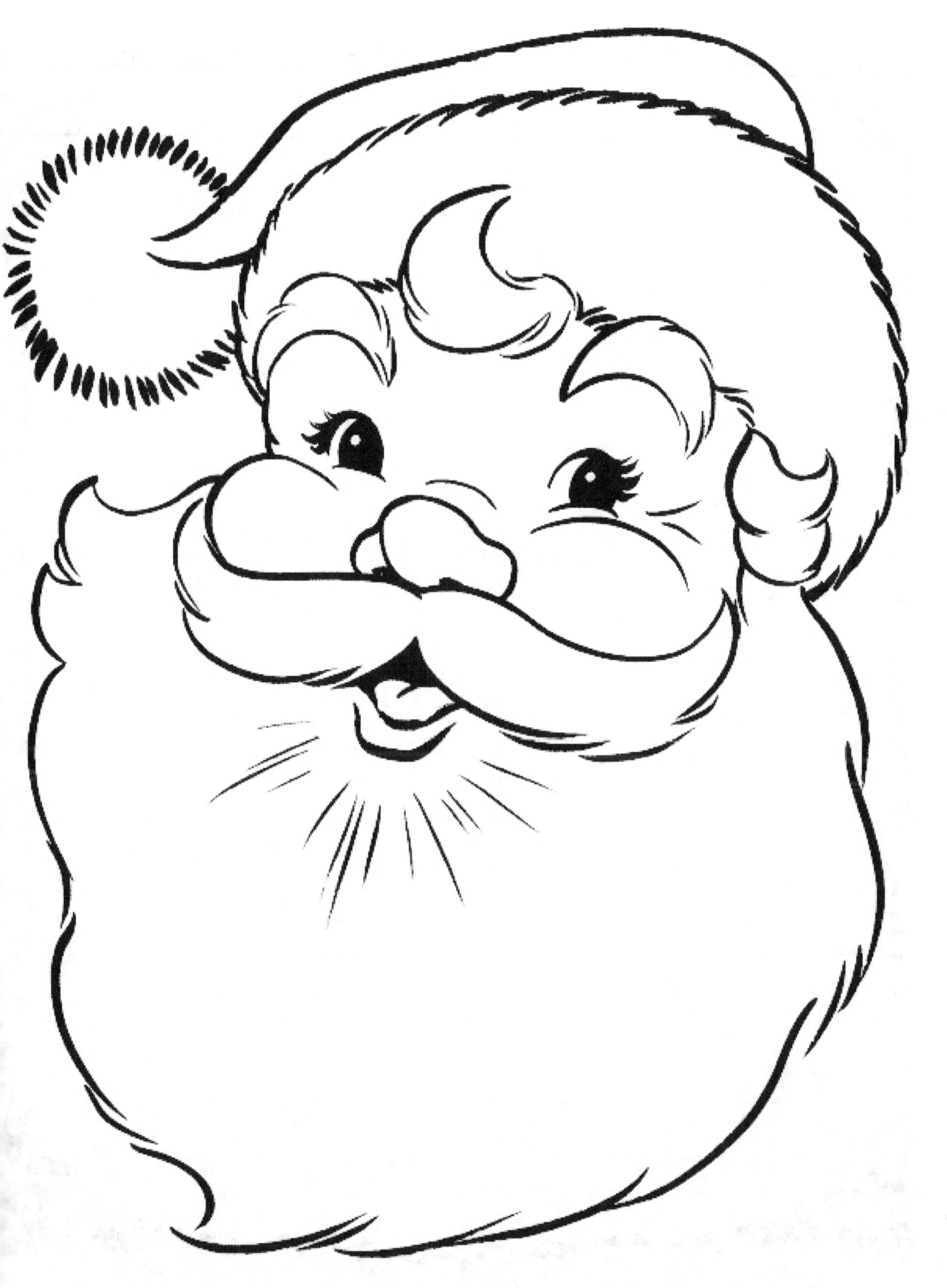

Merry
Christmas

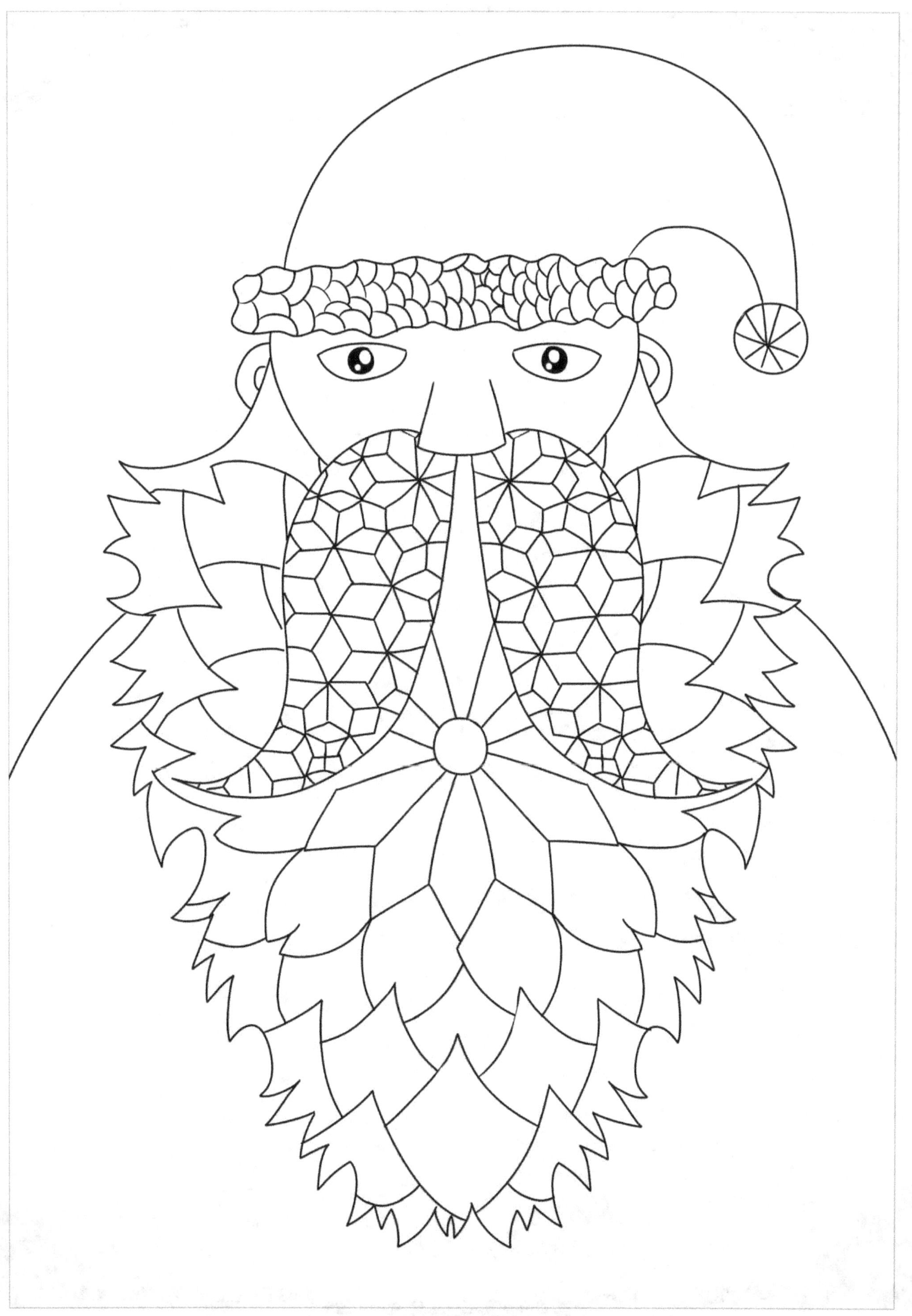

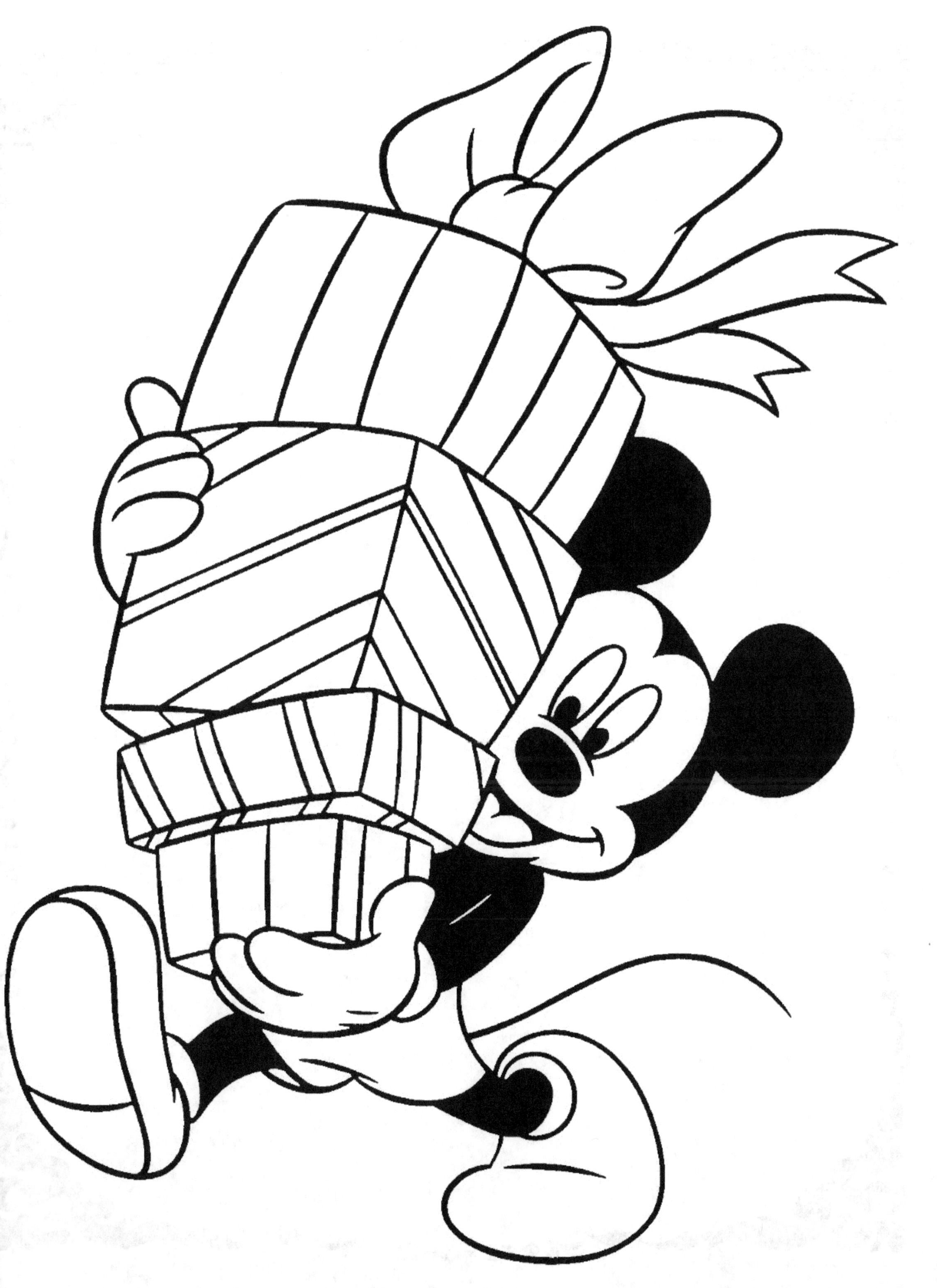

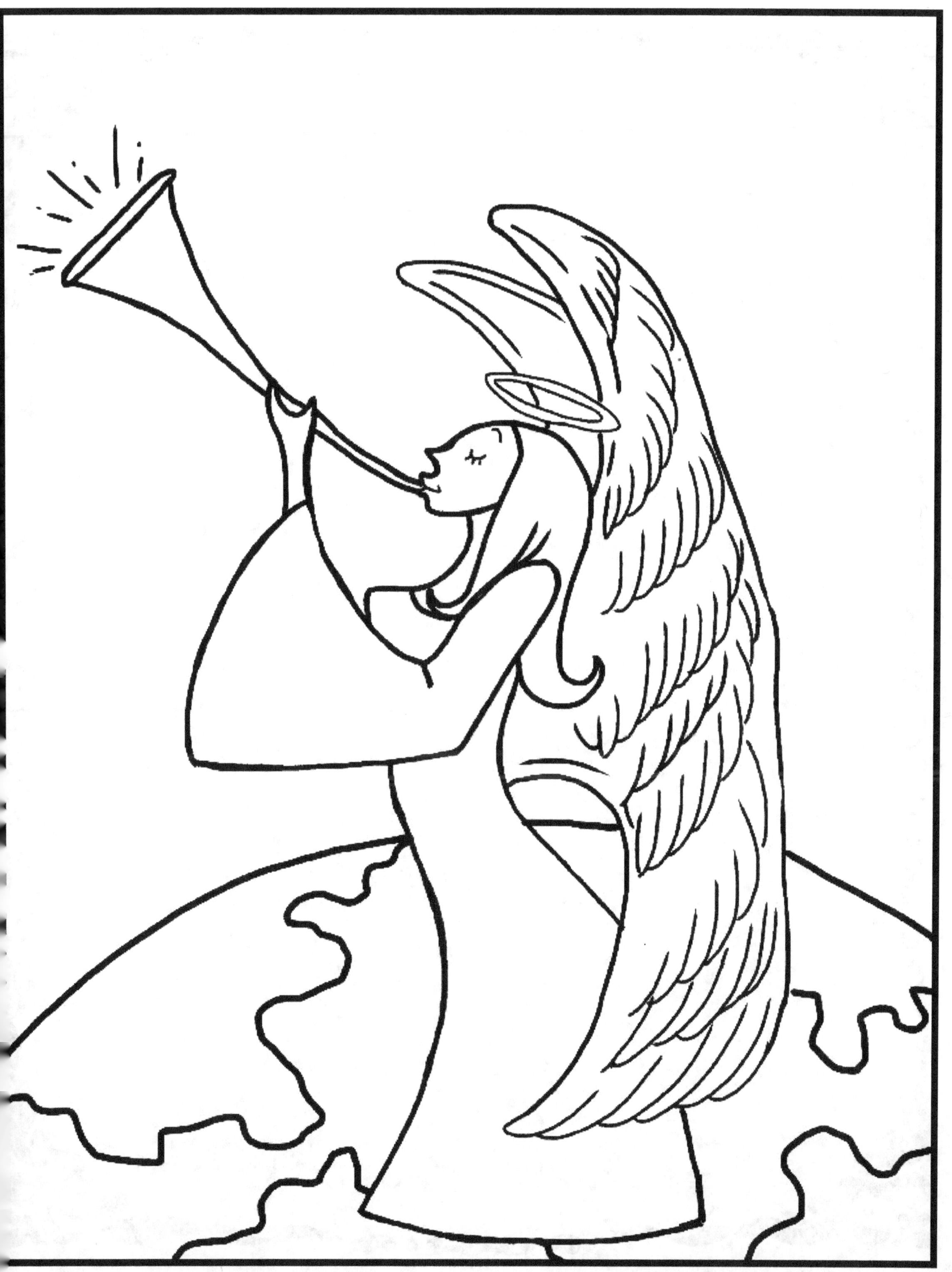

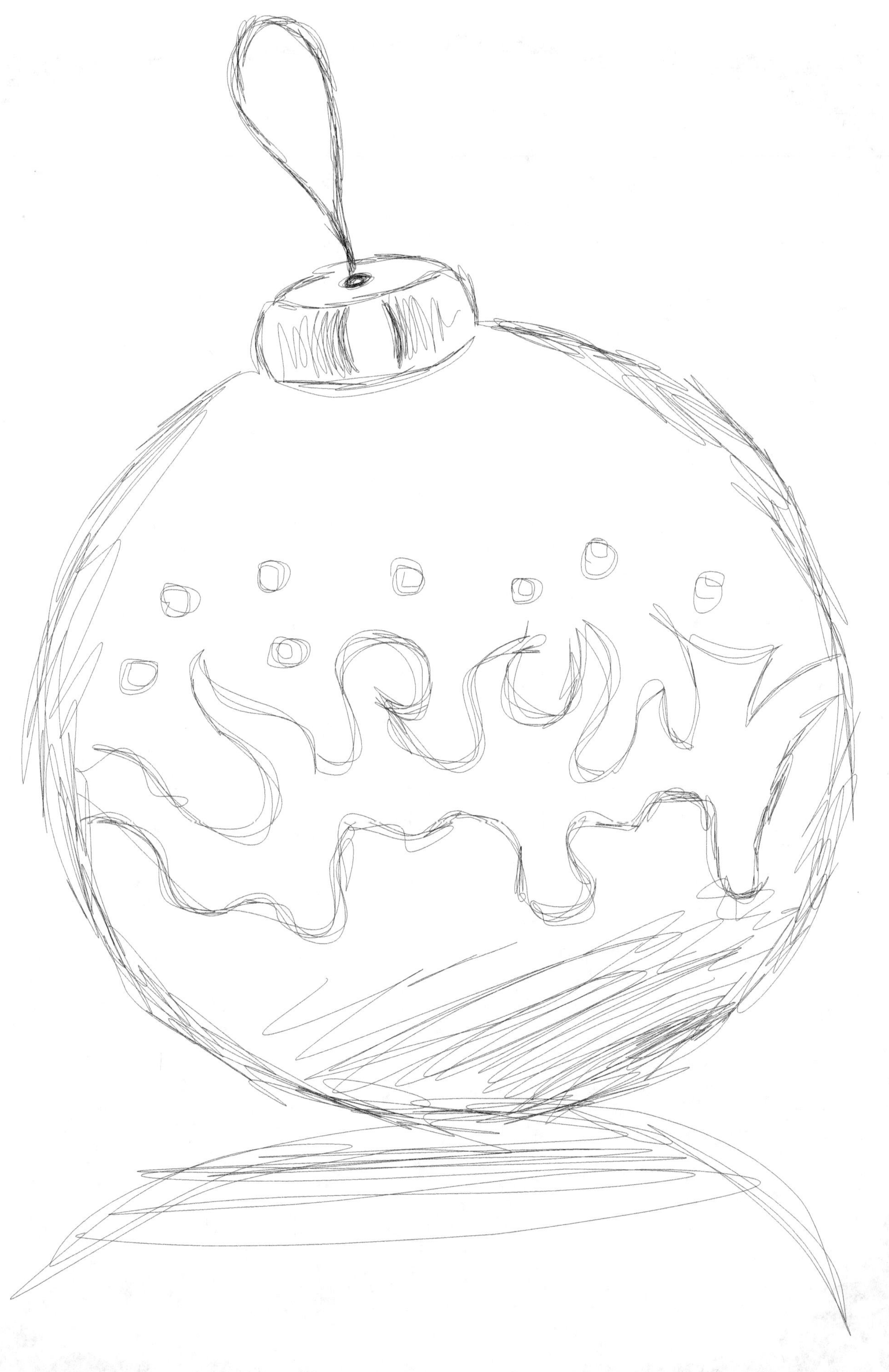

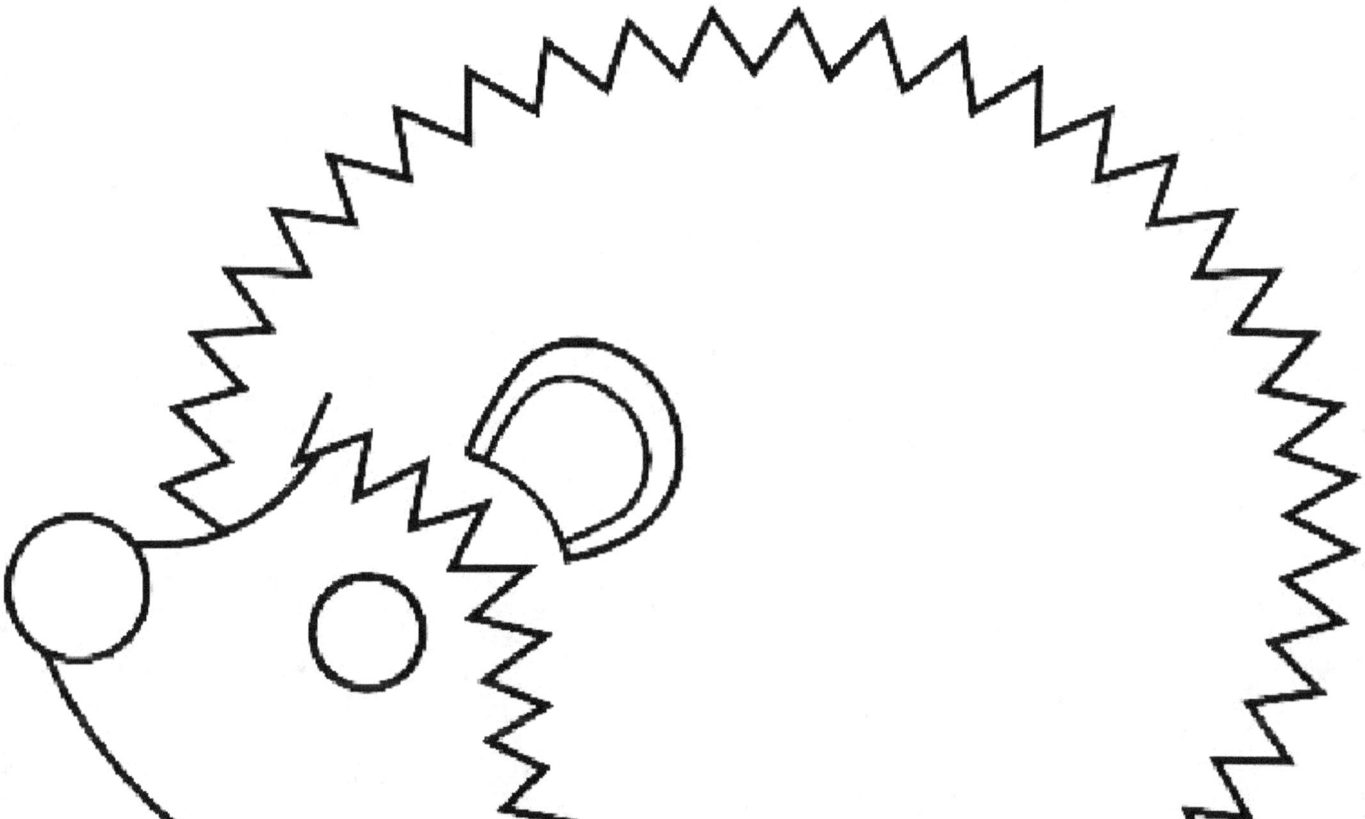

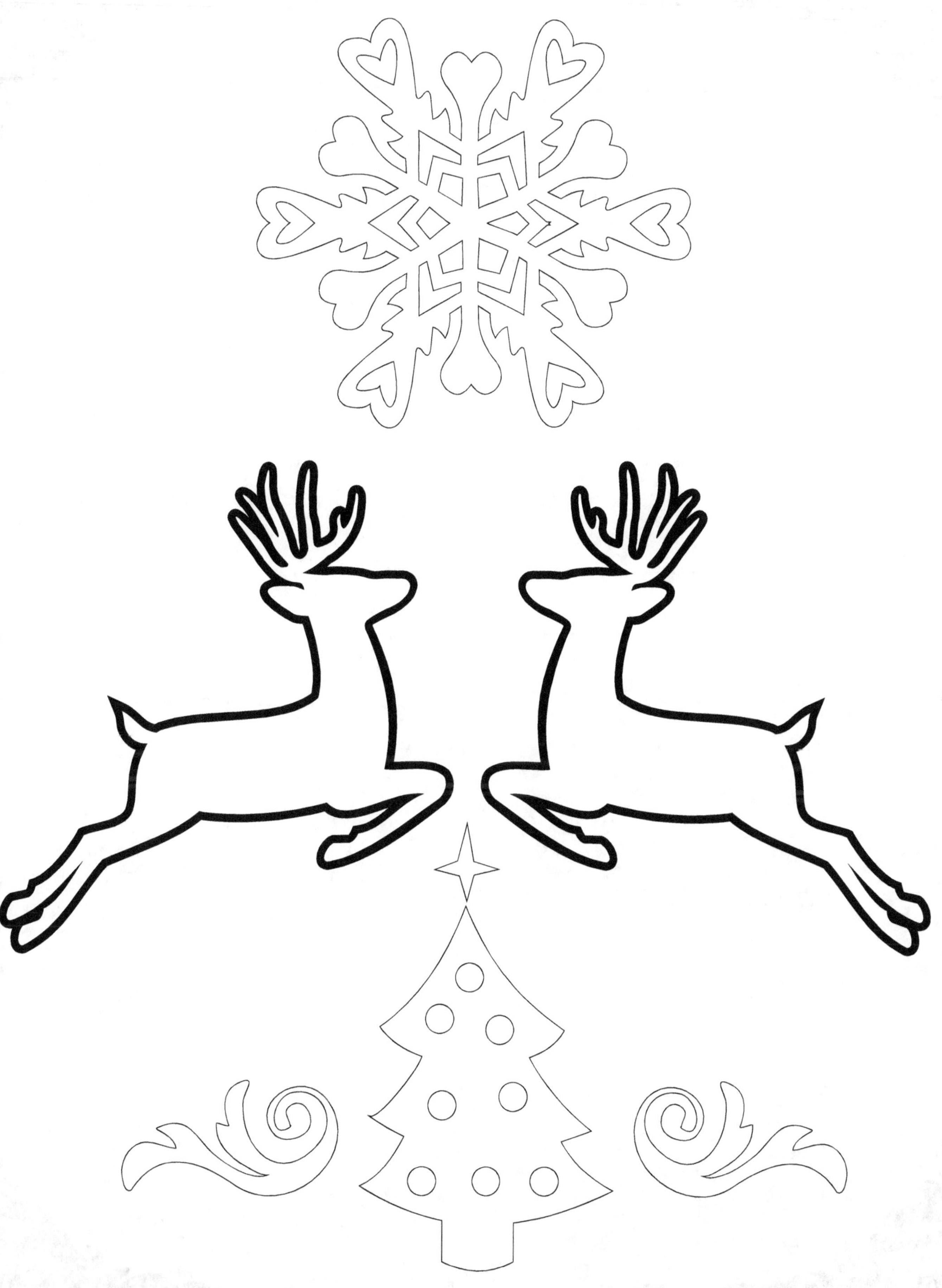

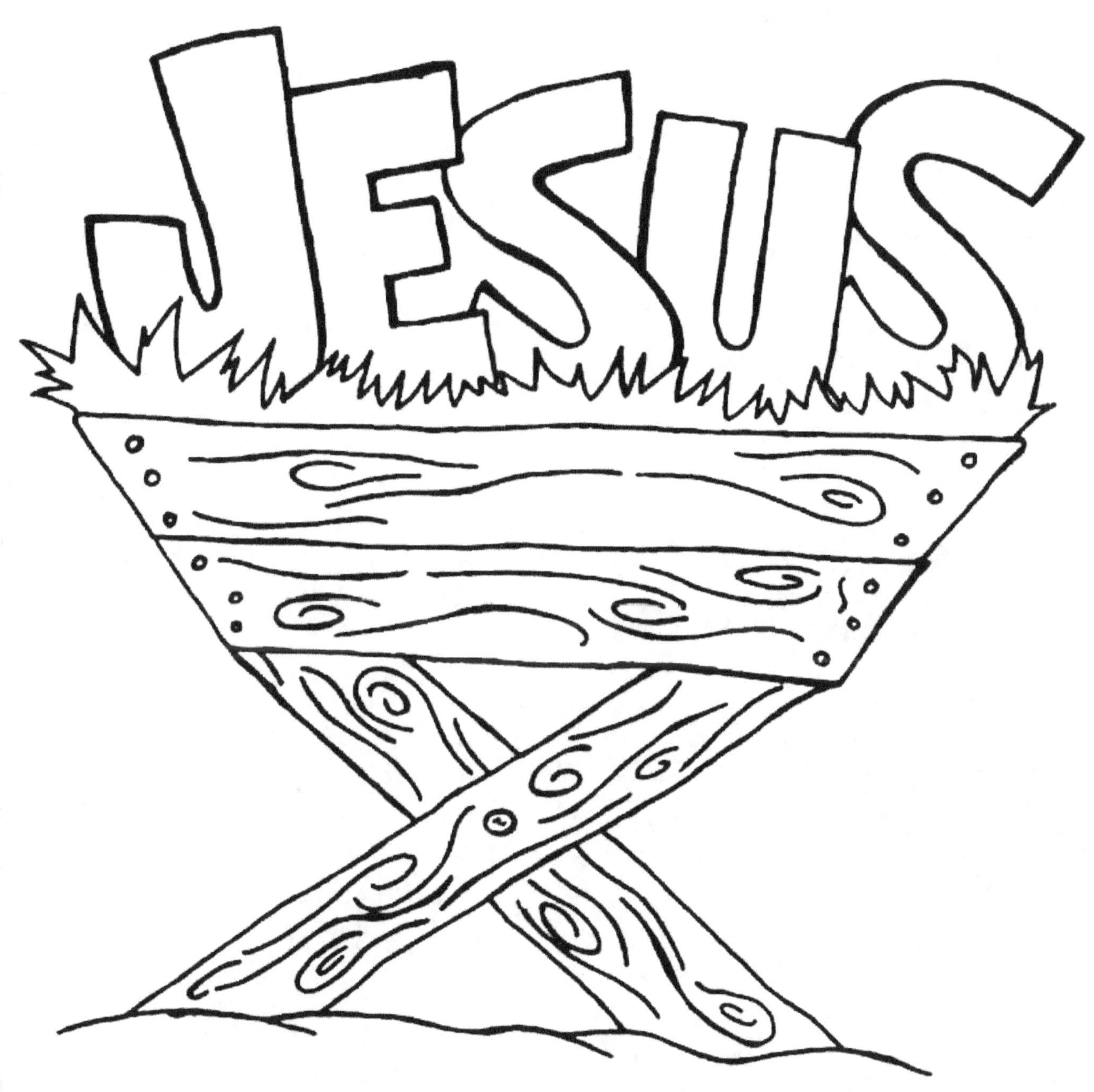
JESUS

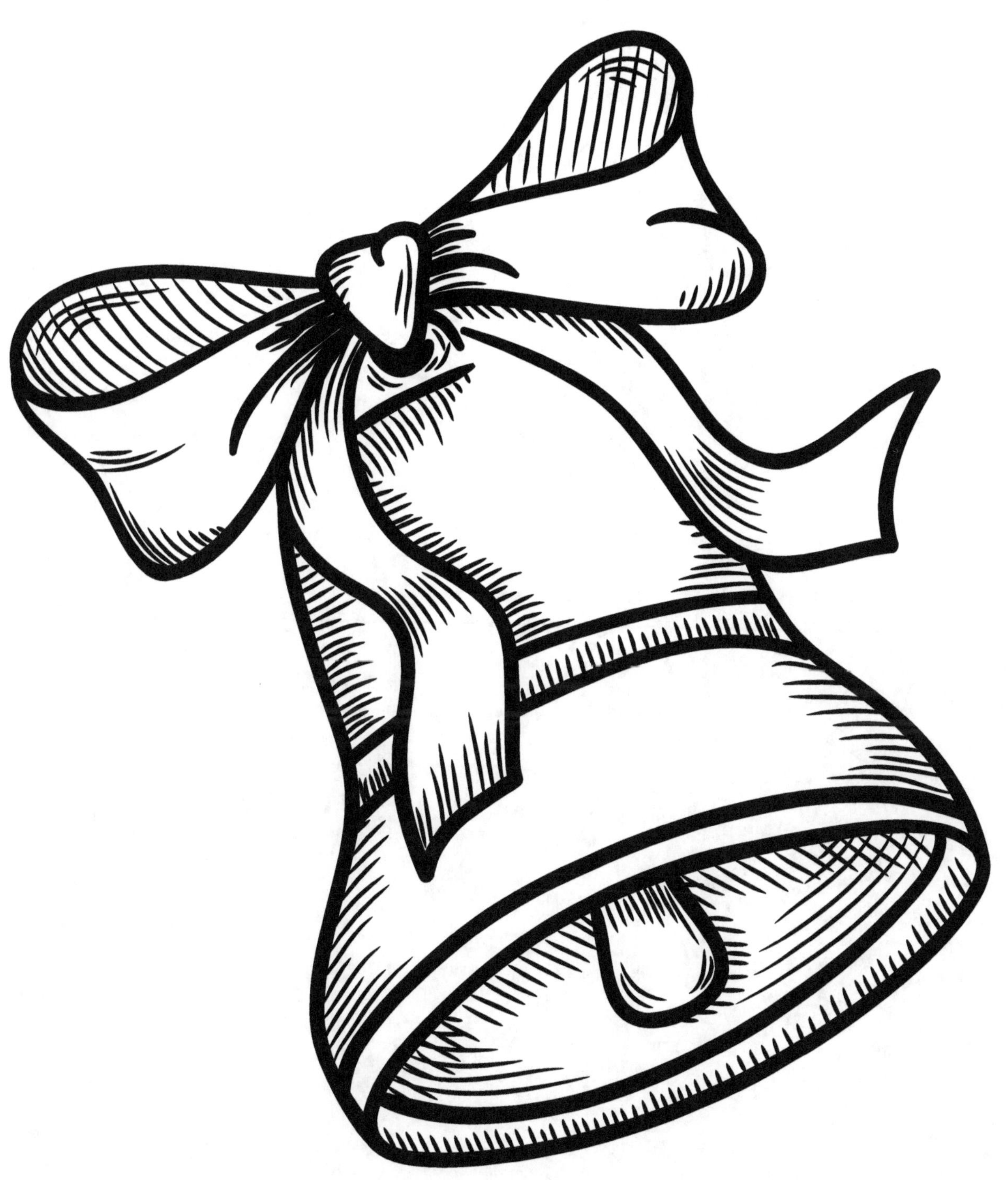

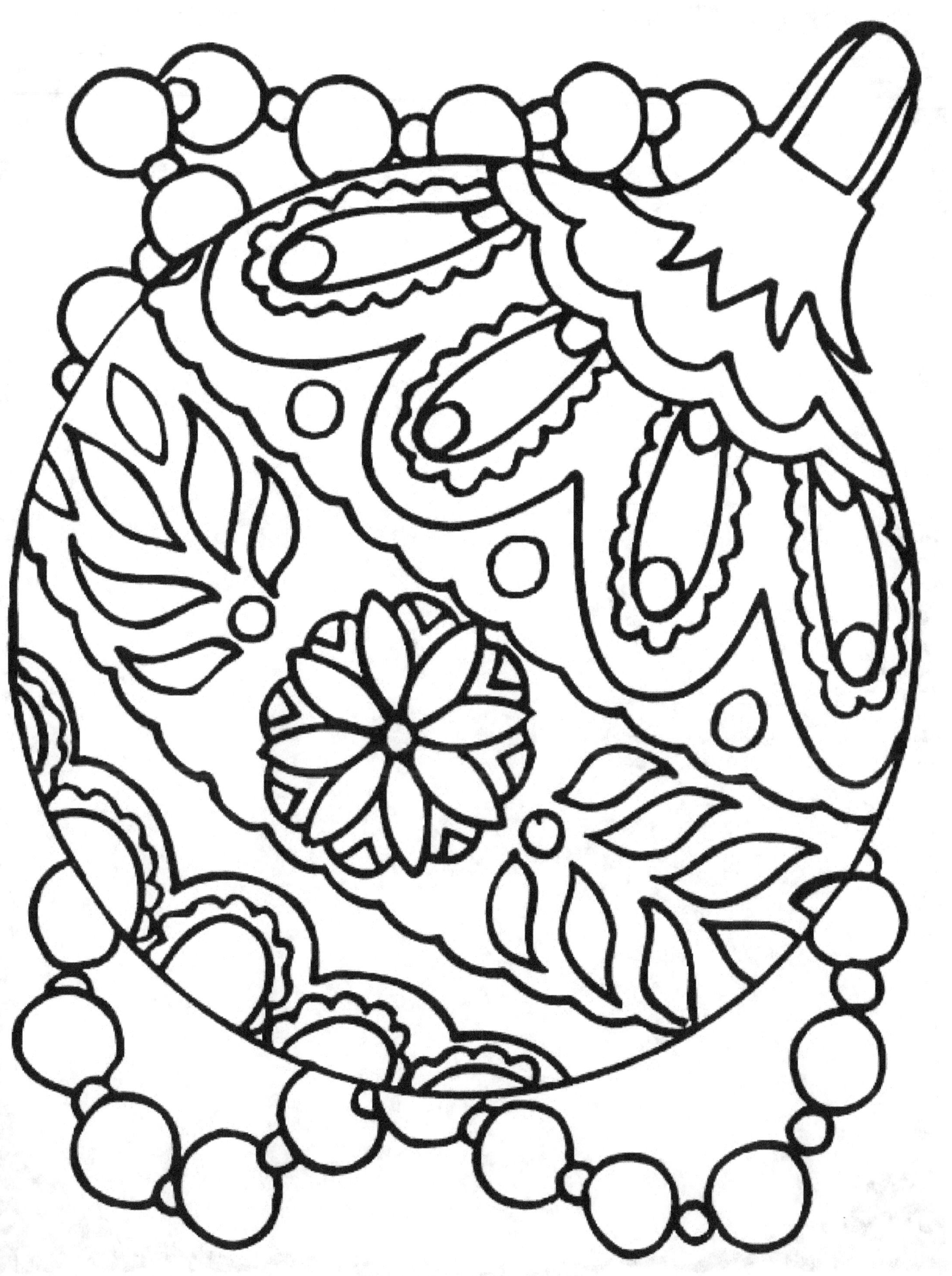

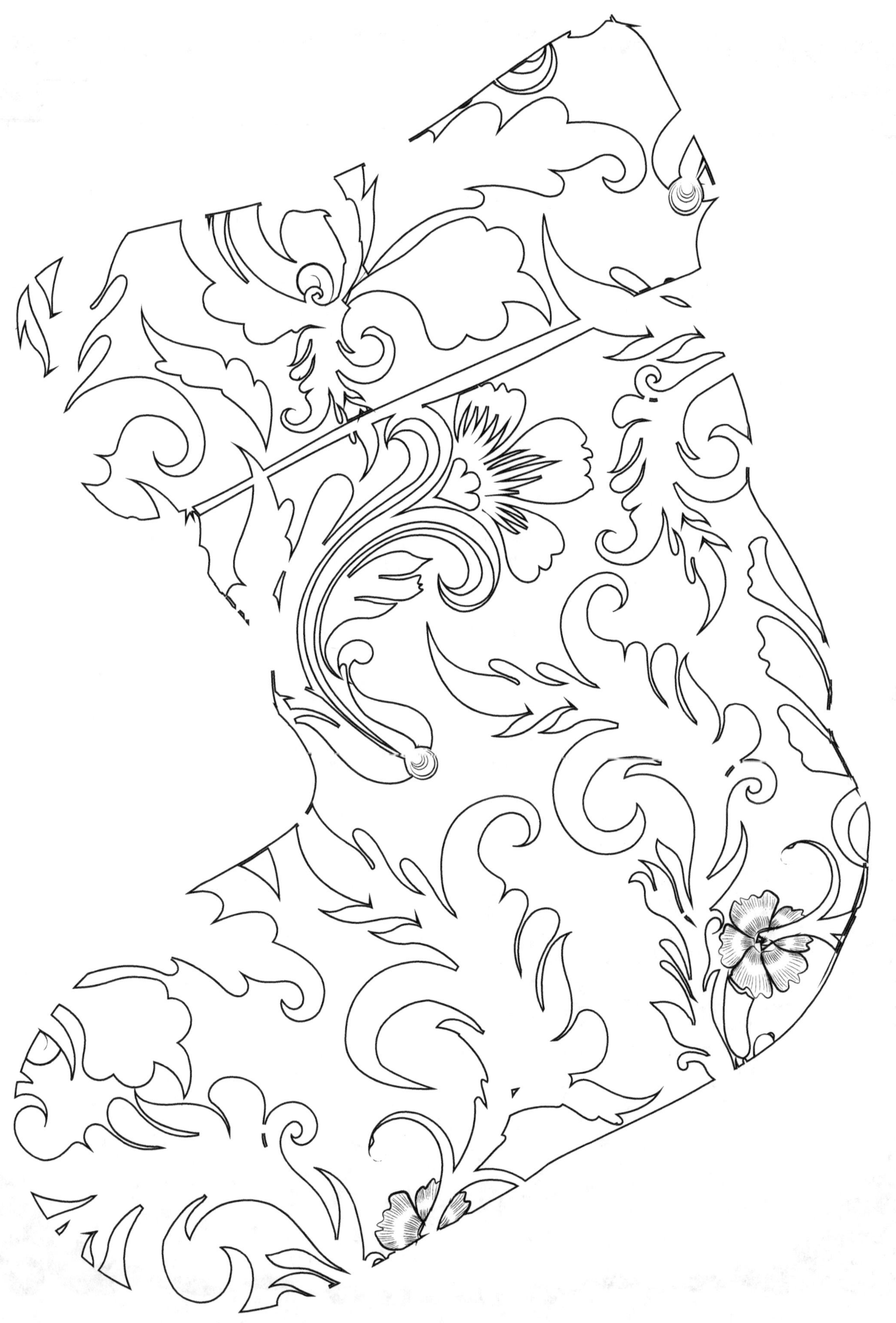

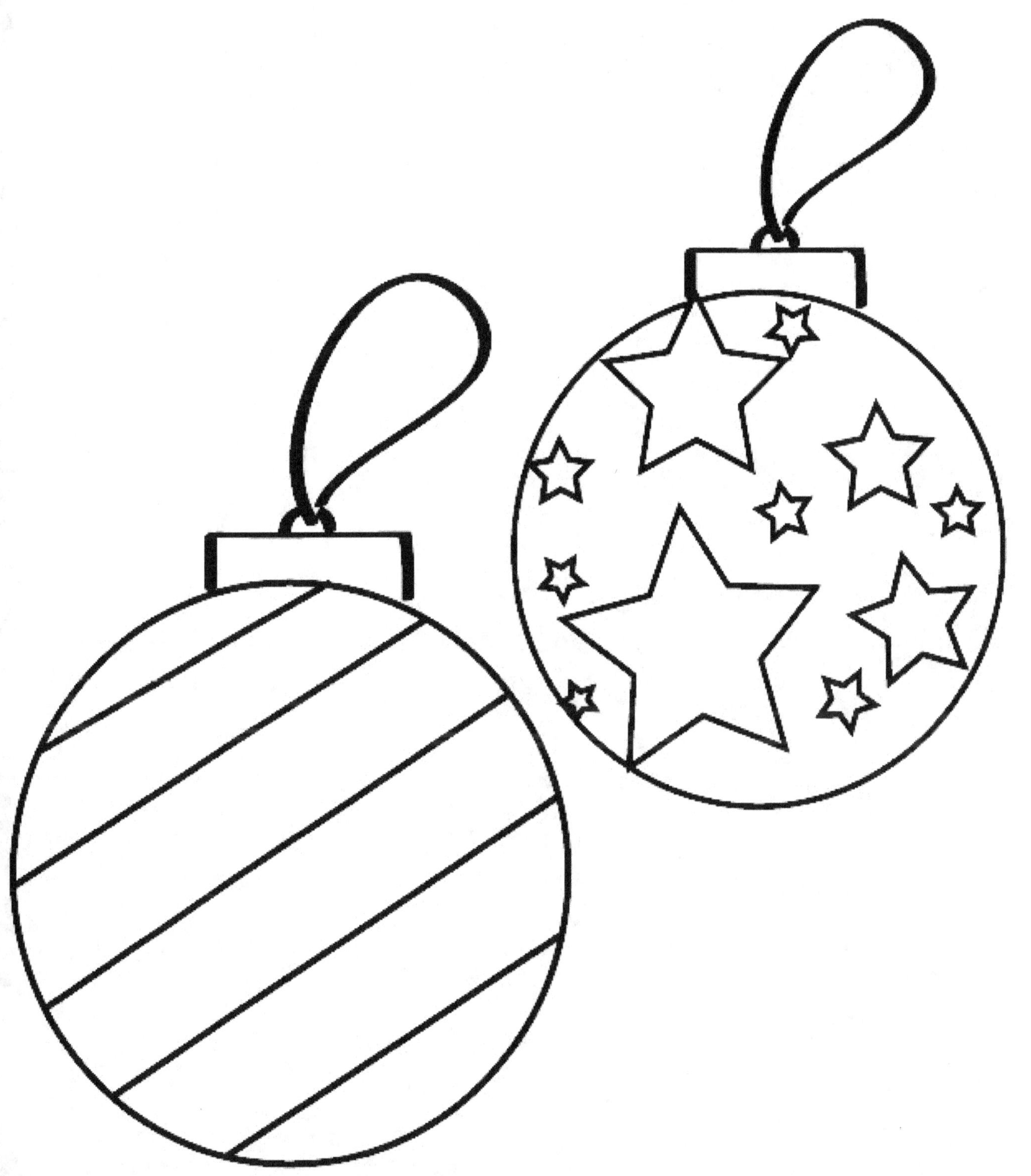

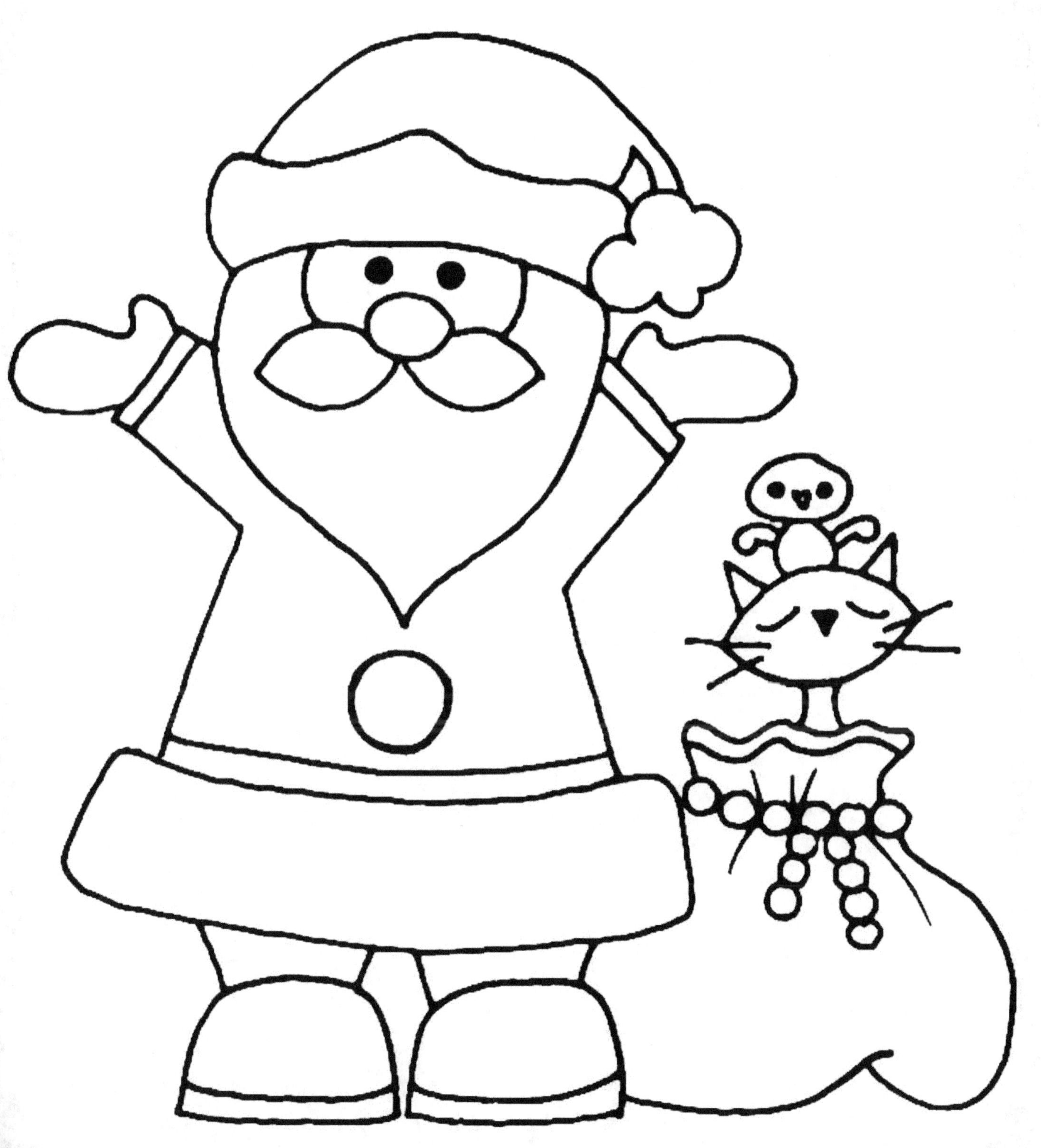

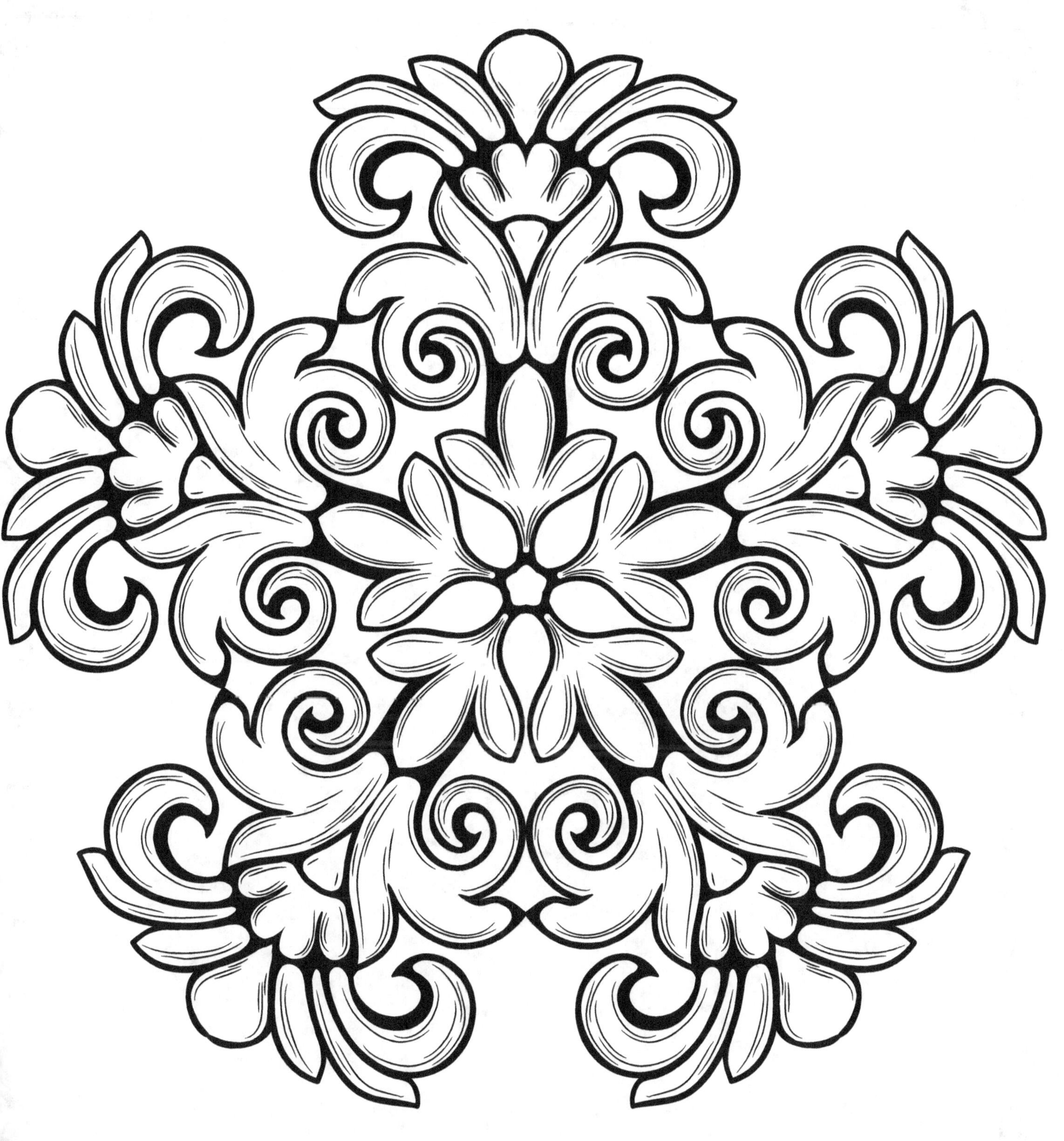

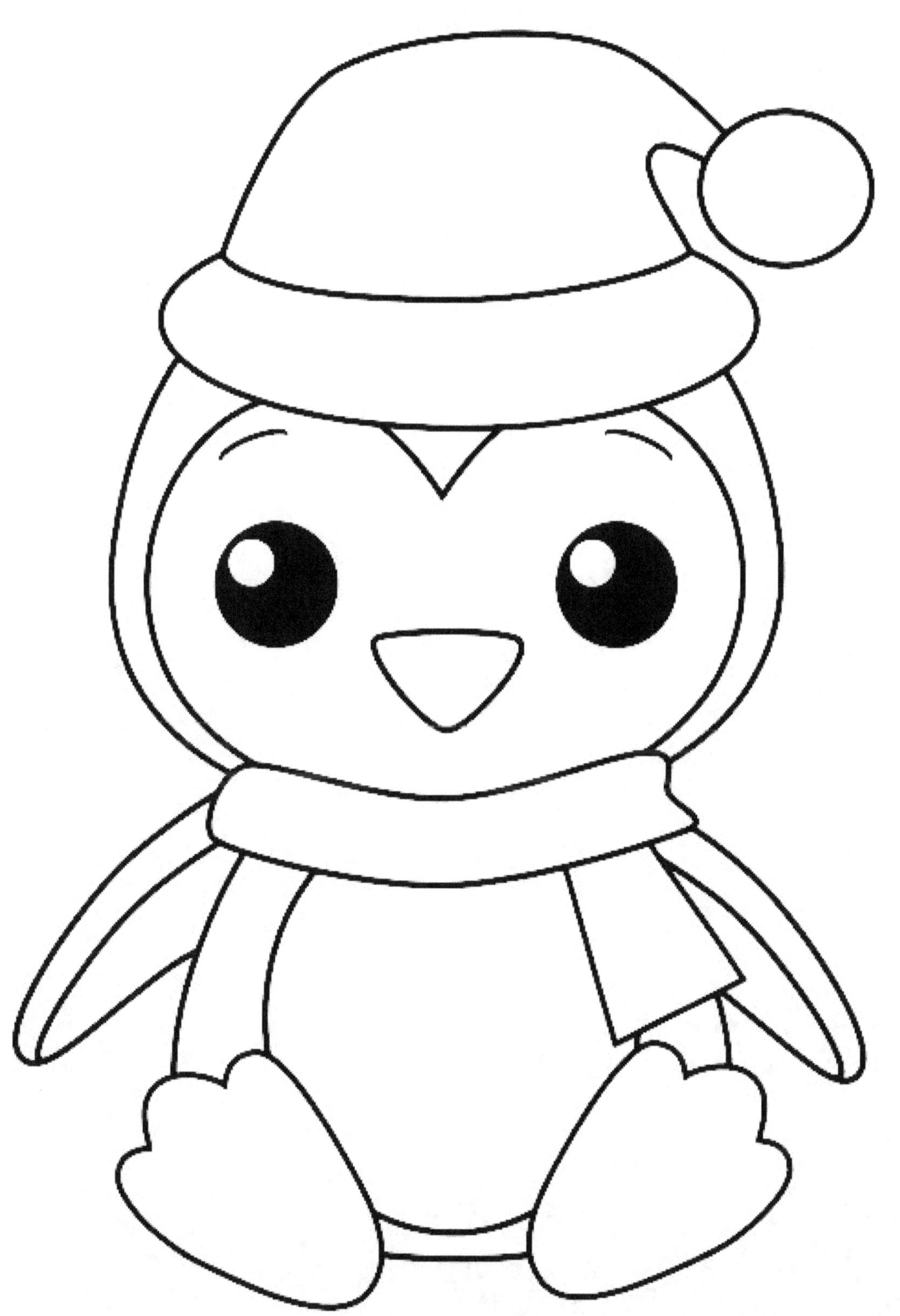

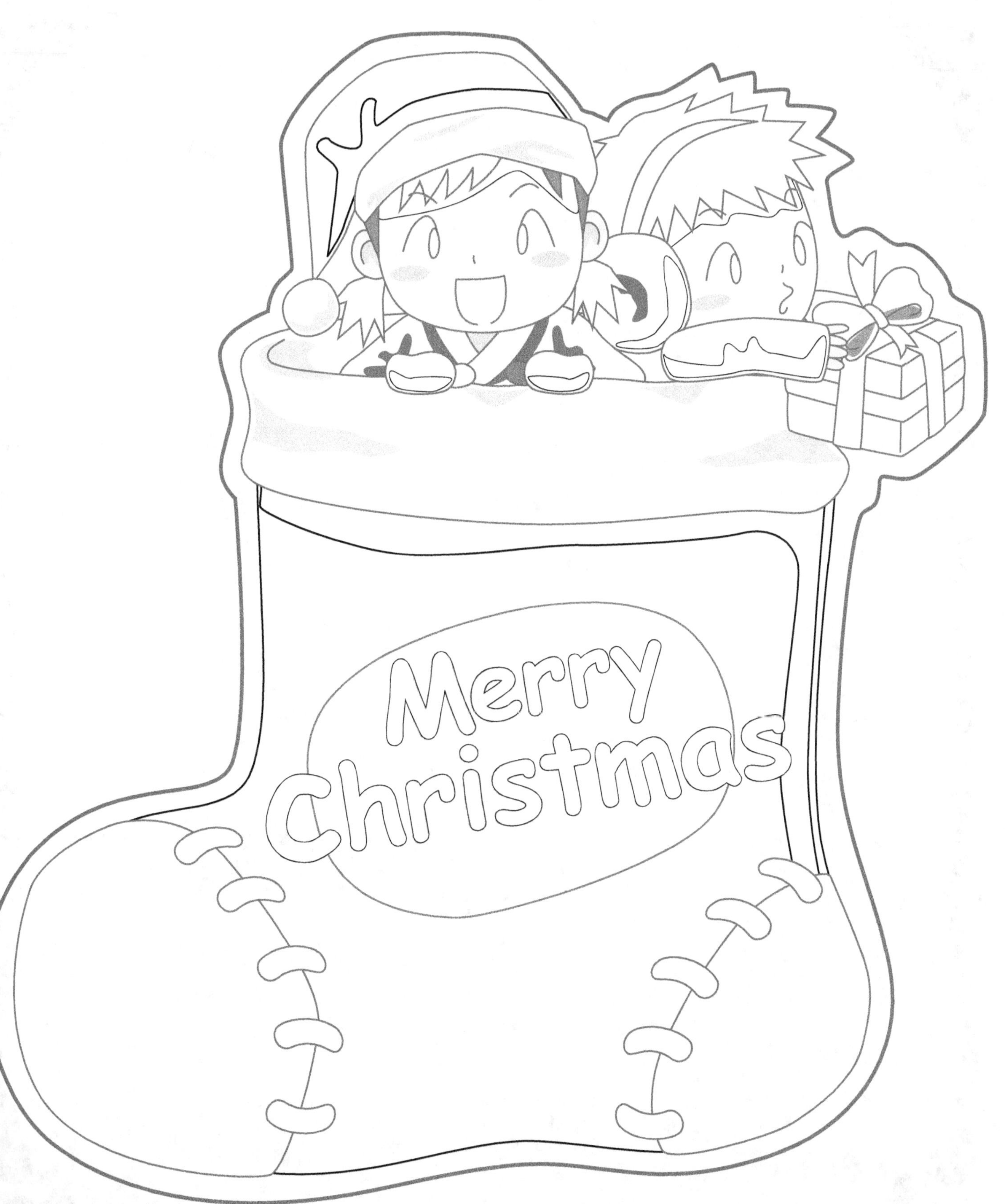

Merry
Christmas

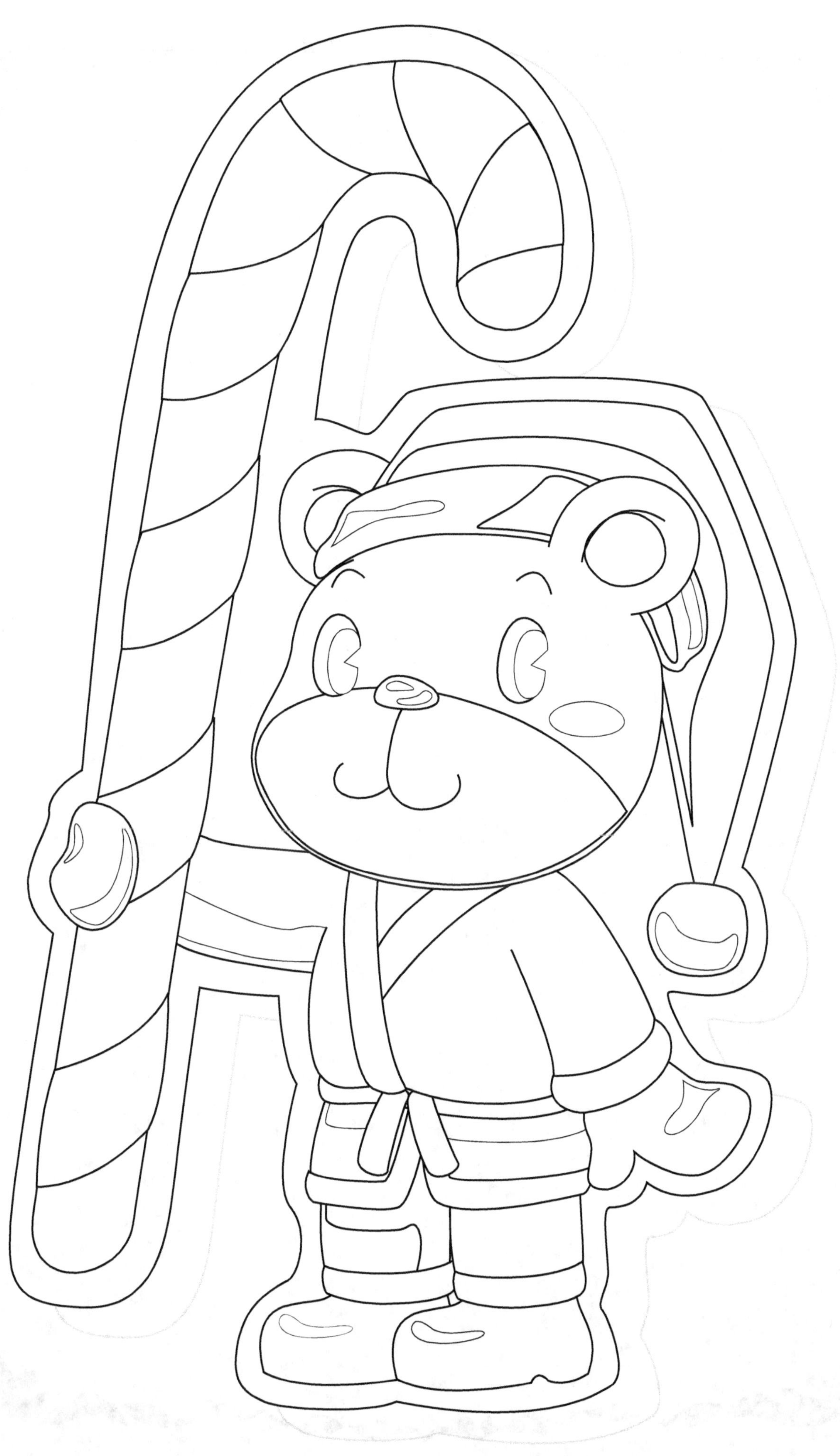

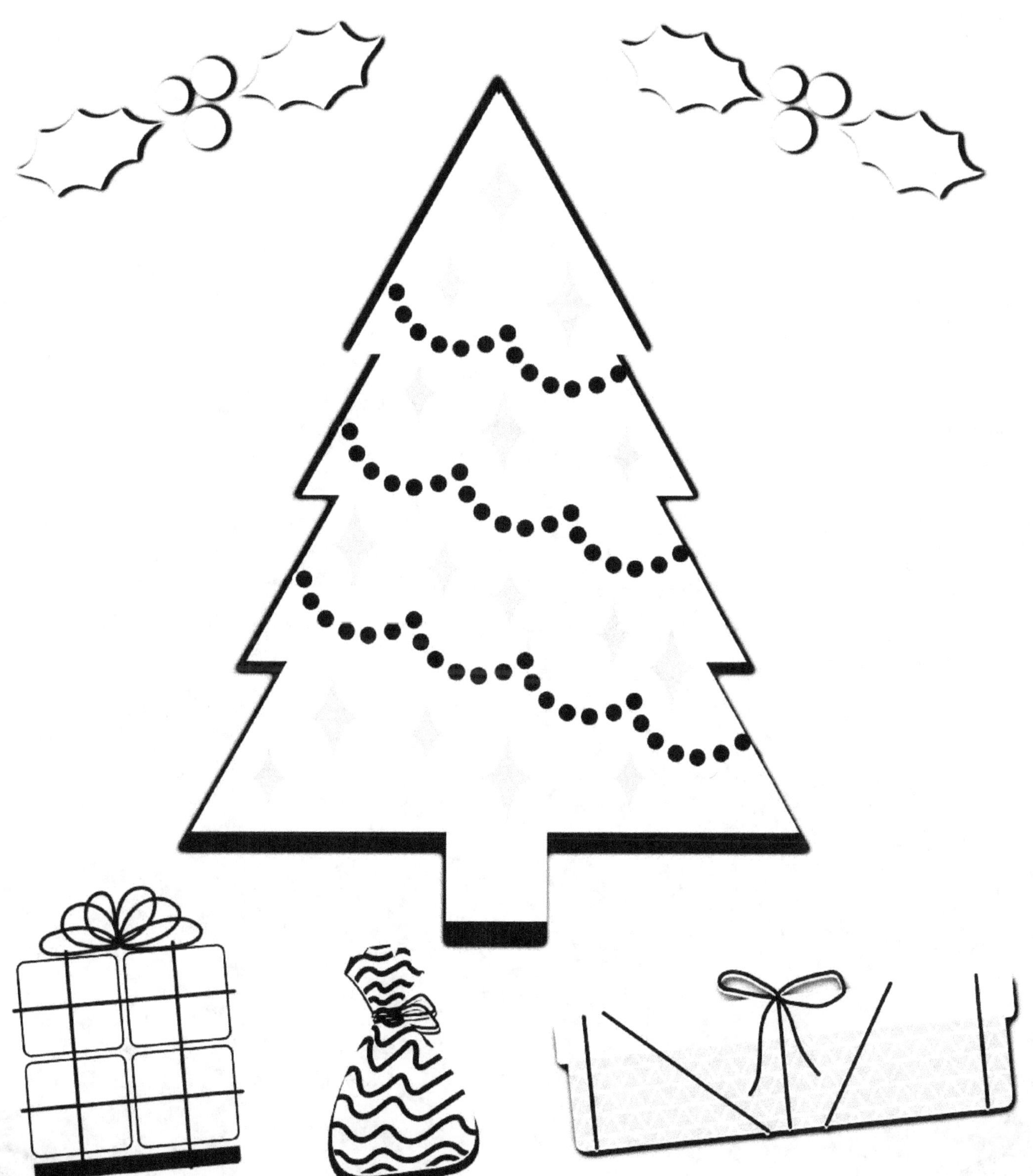

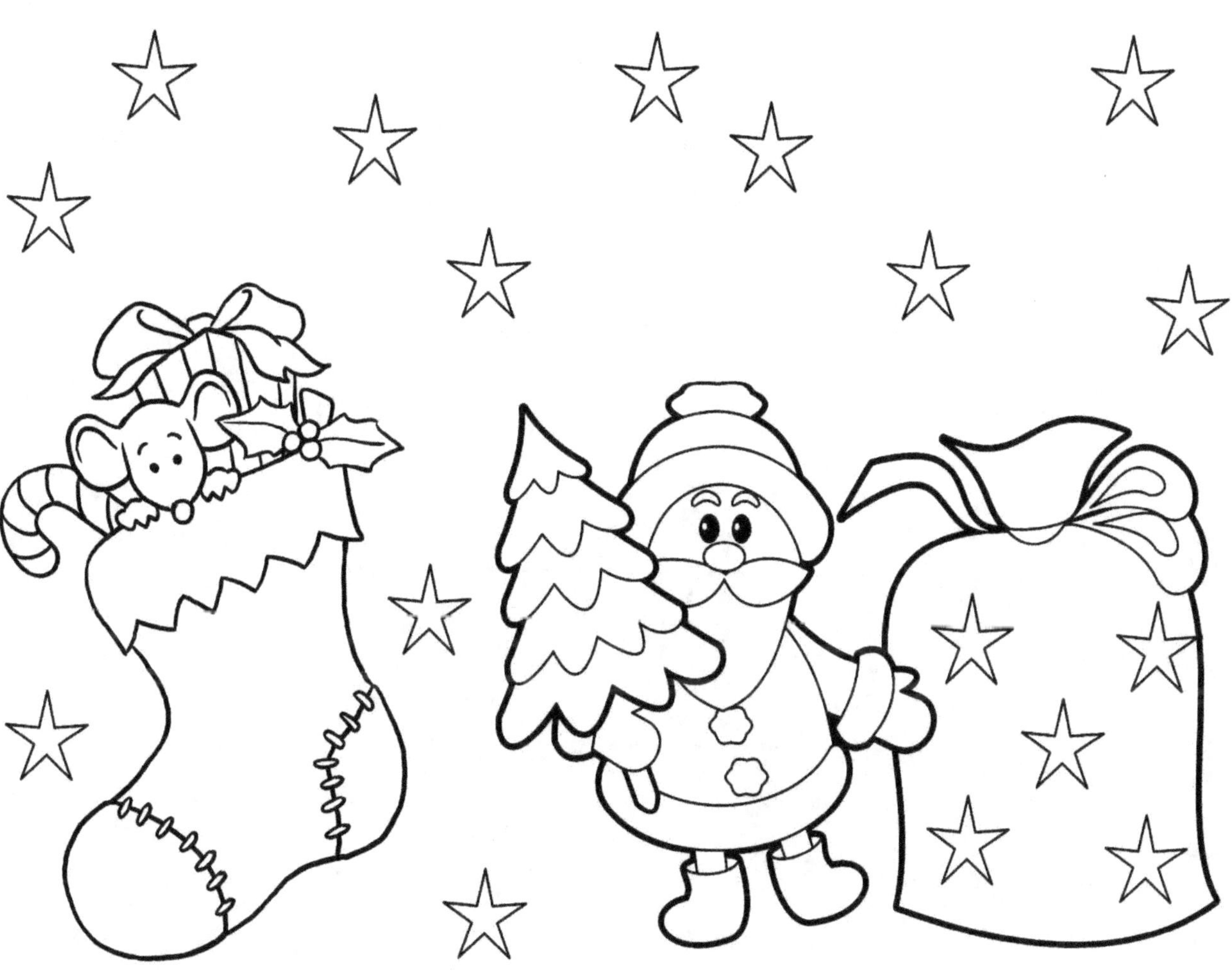

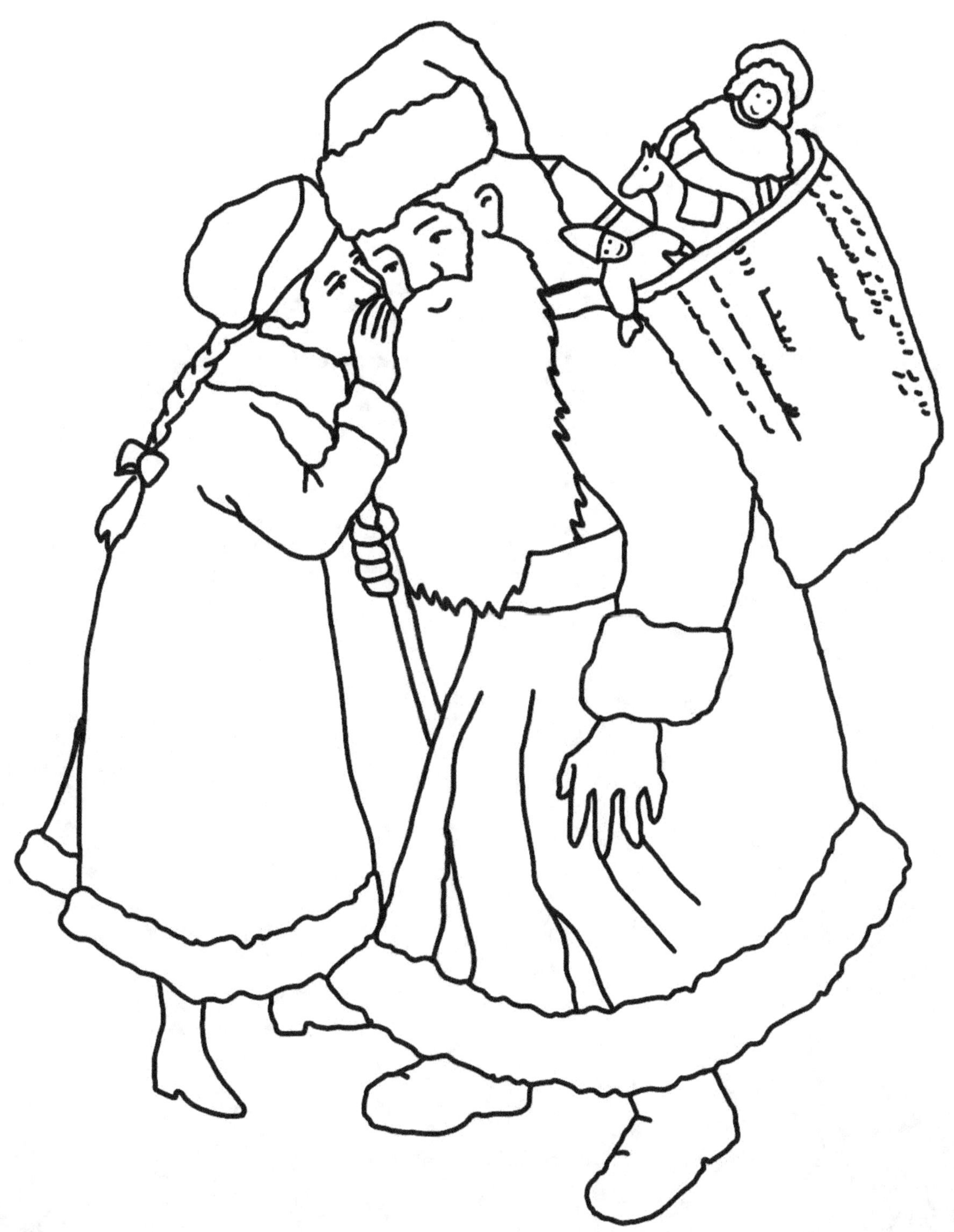

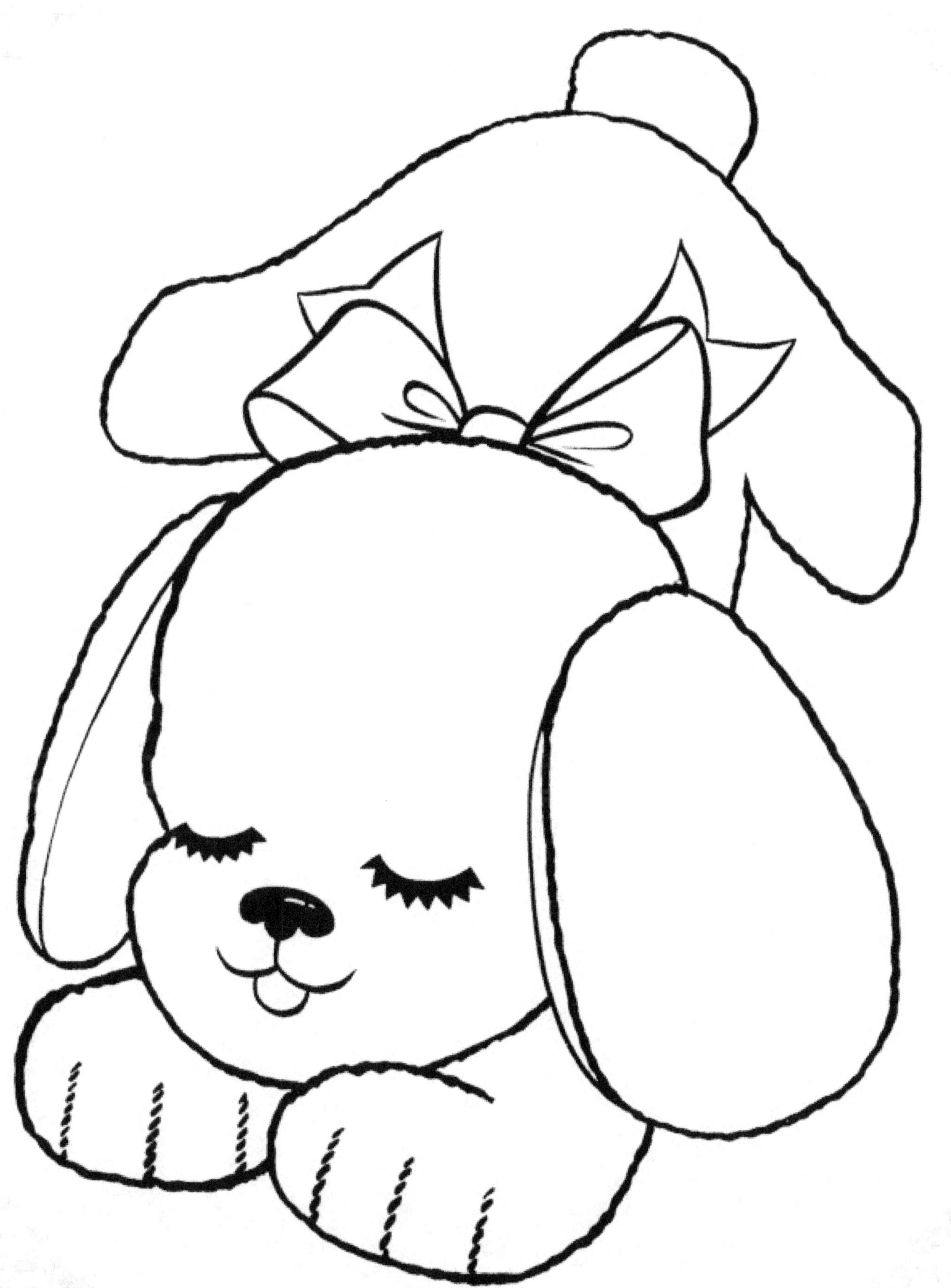

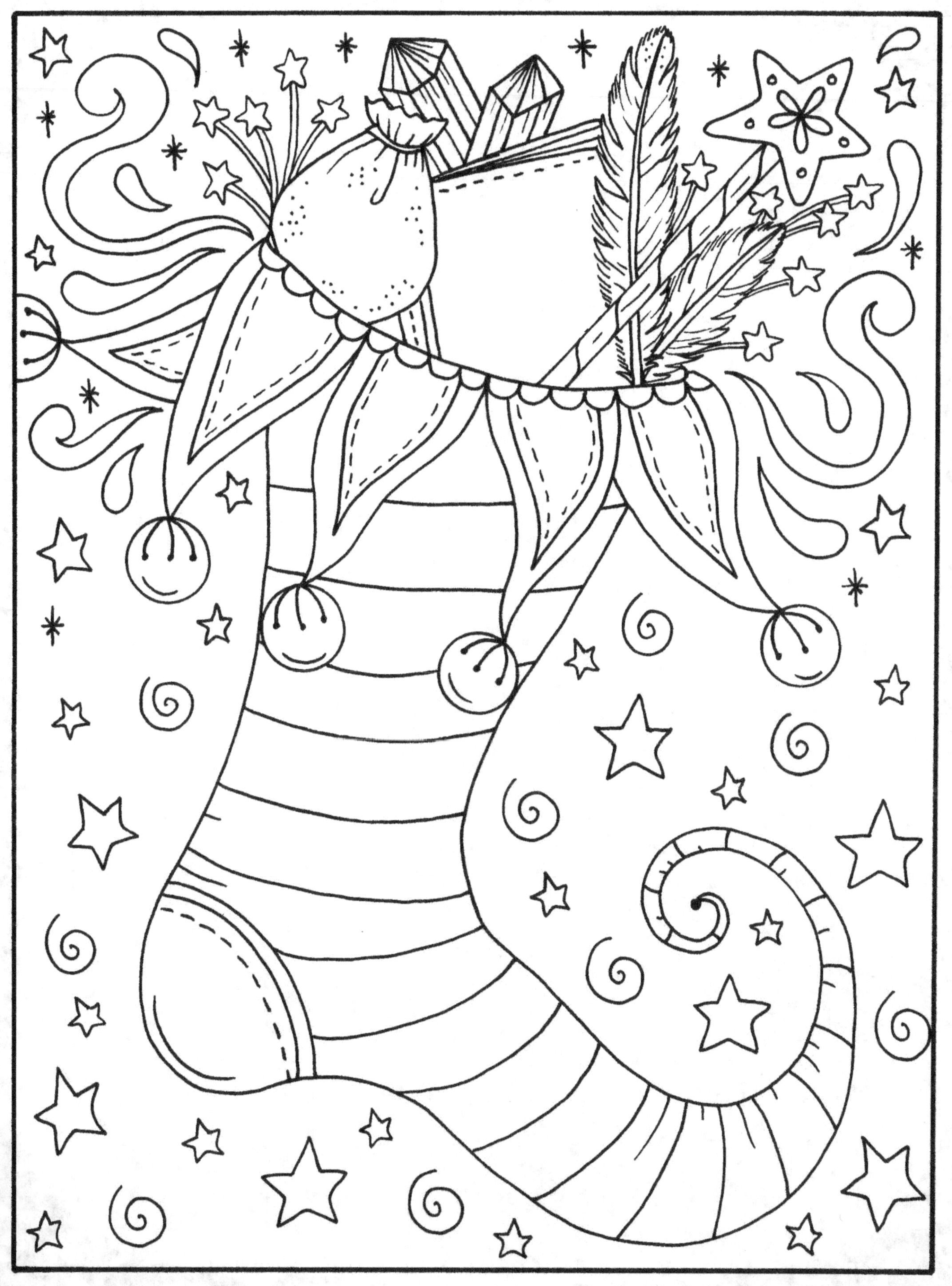

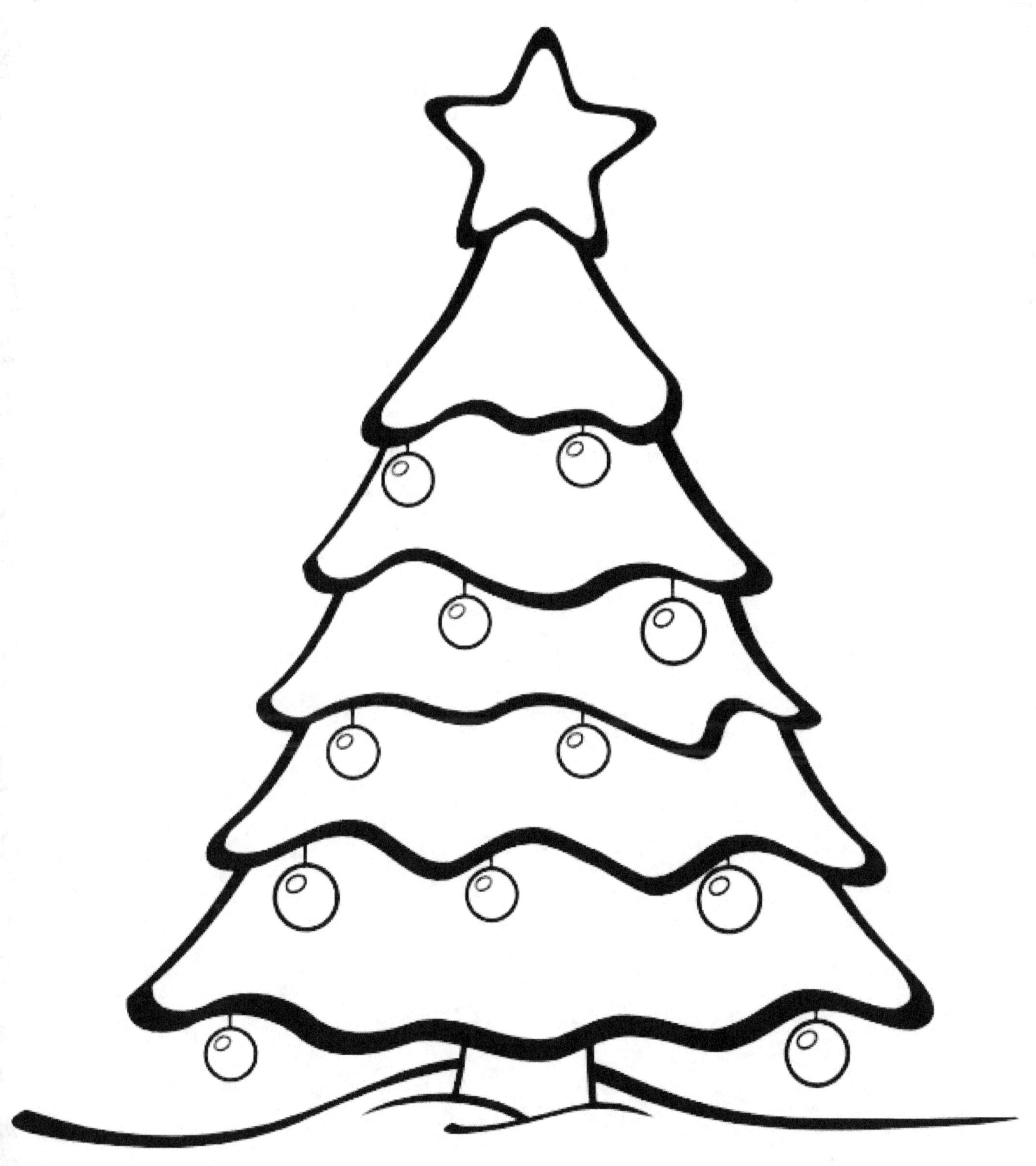

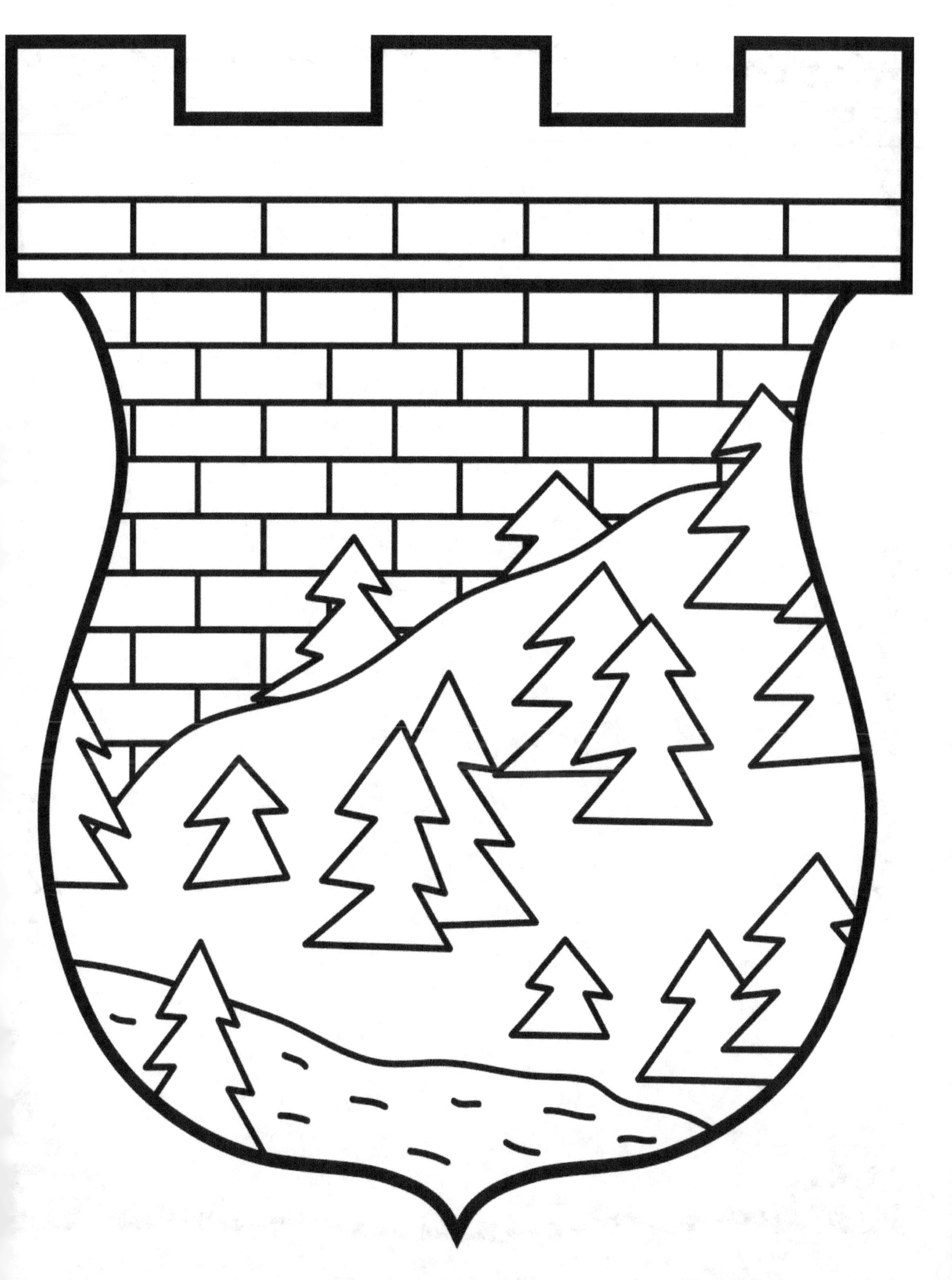

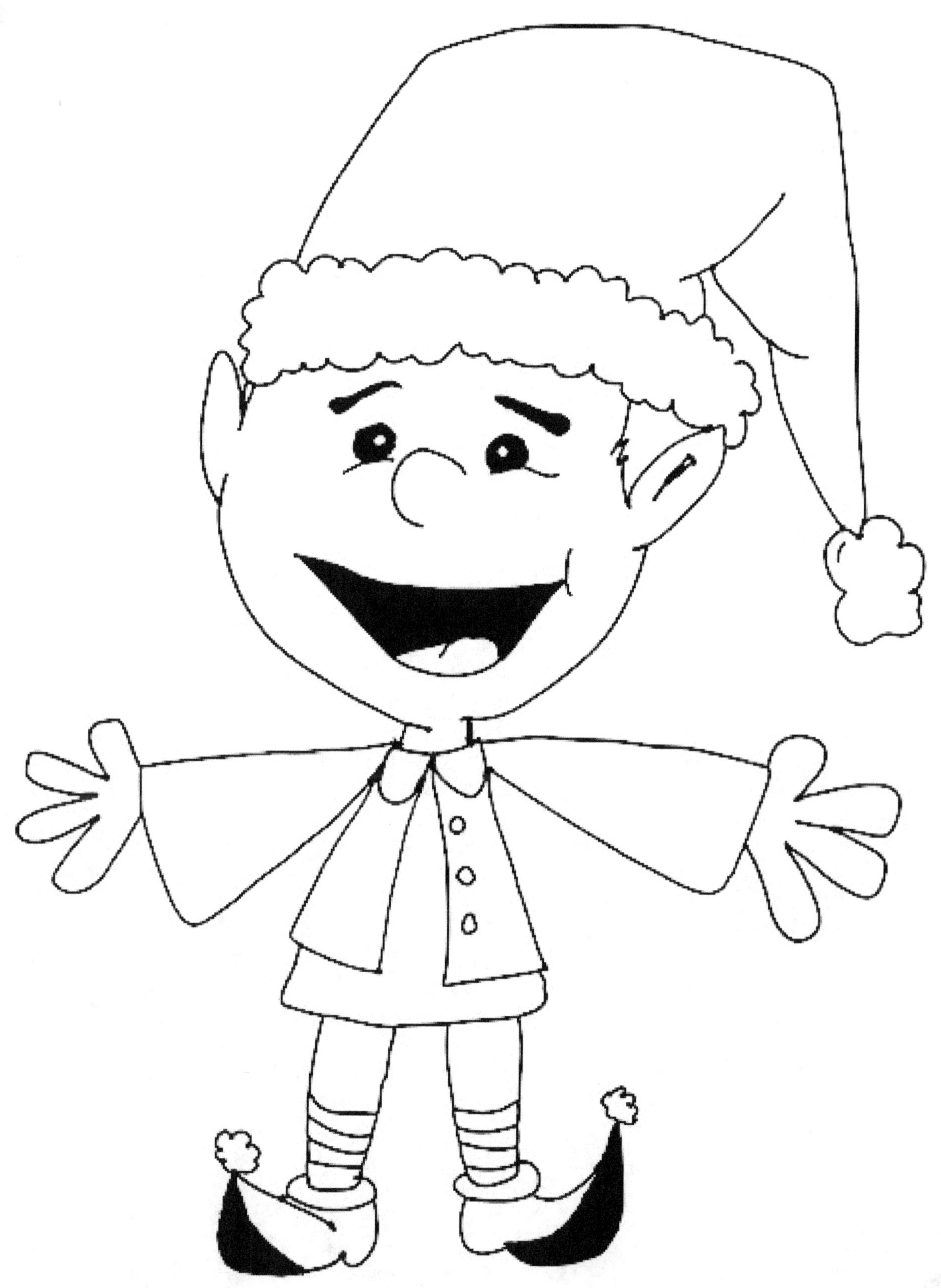

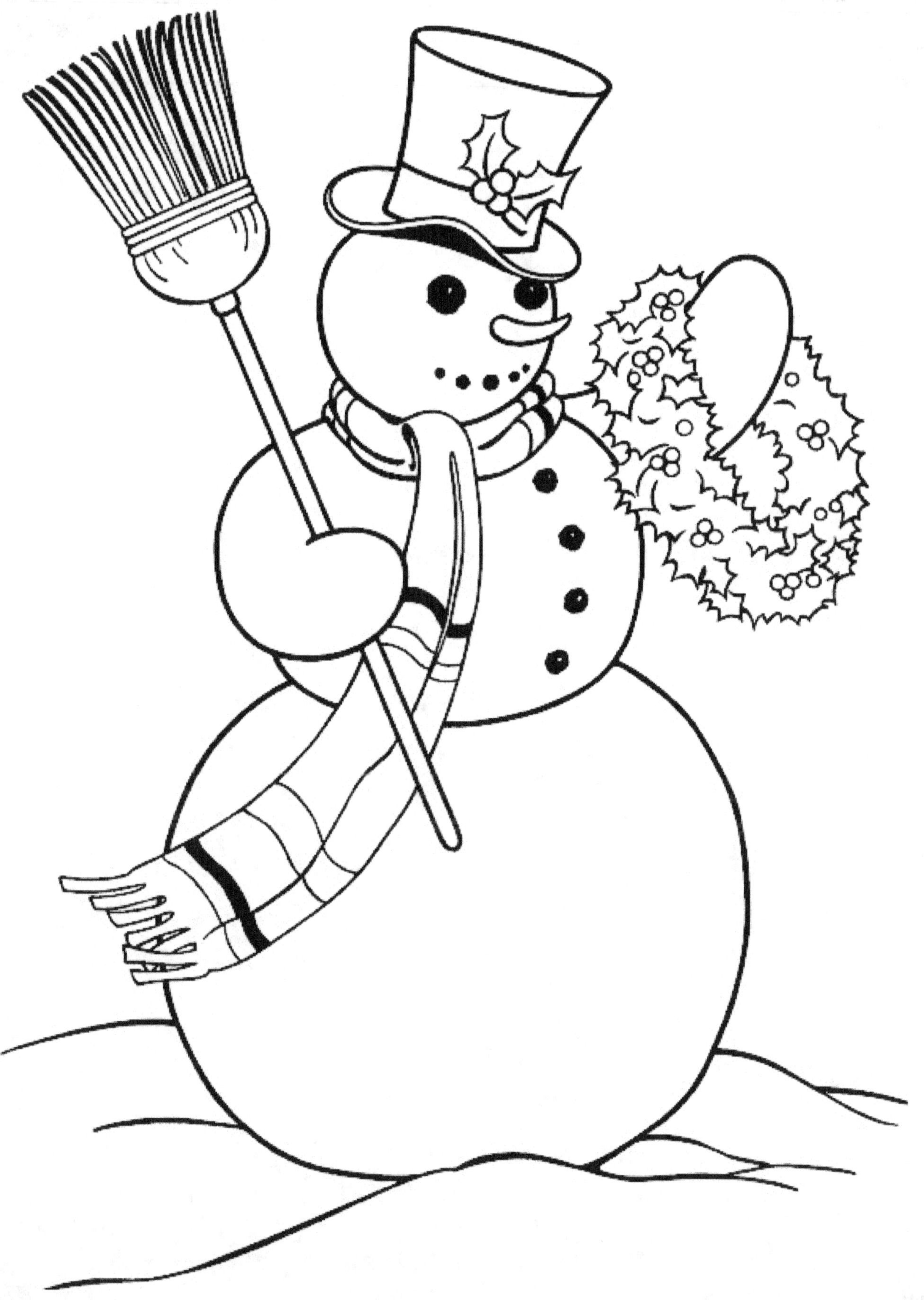

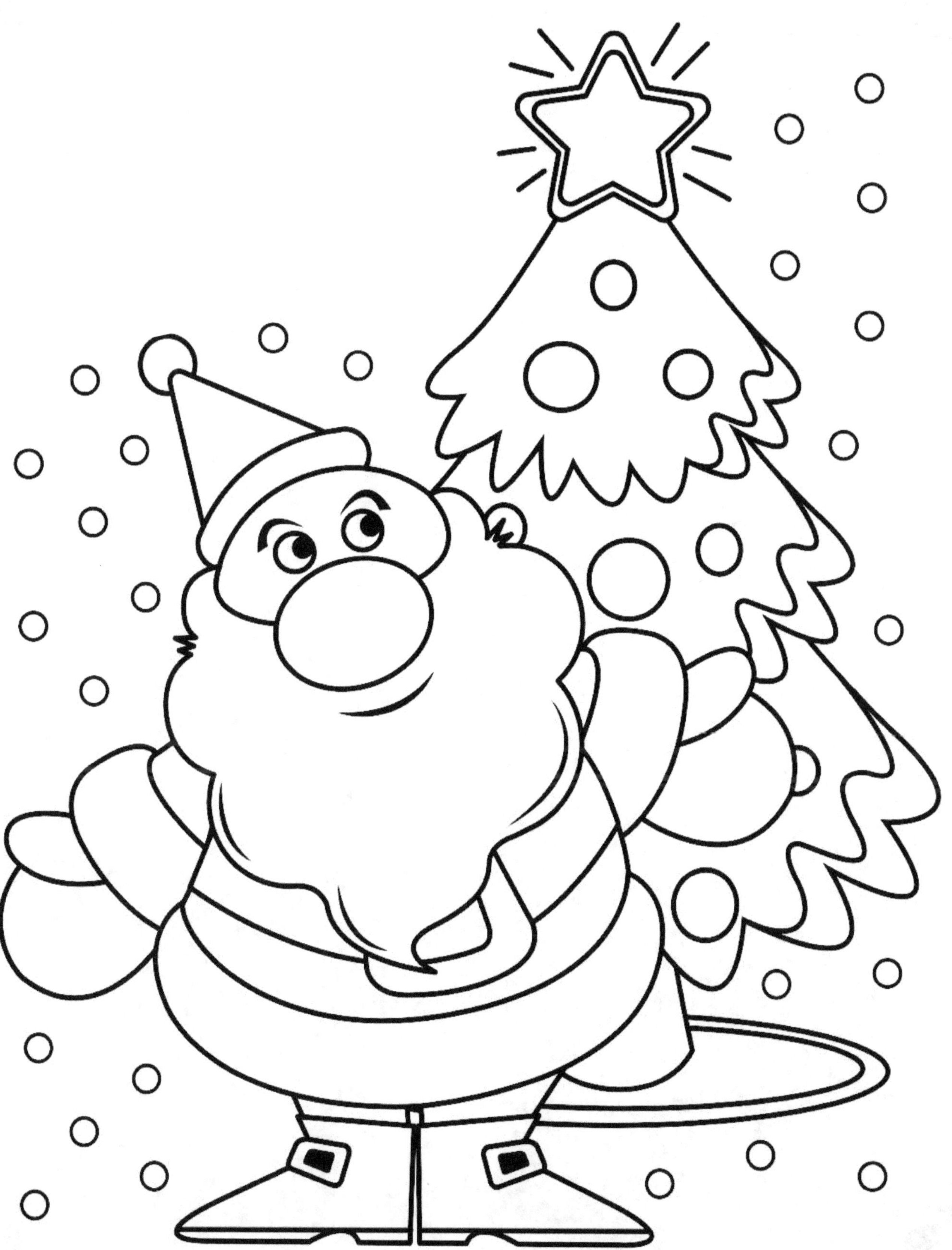

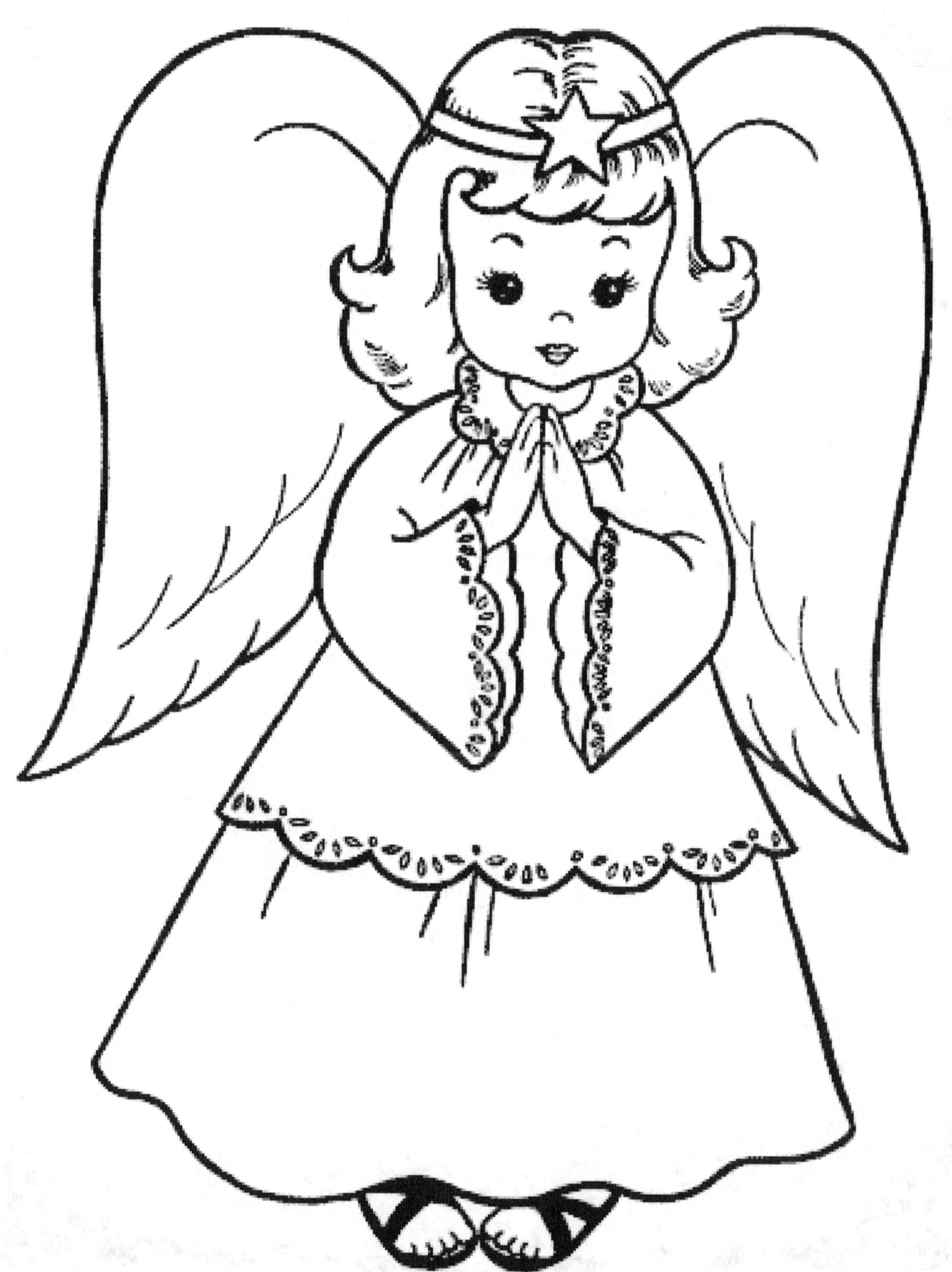

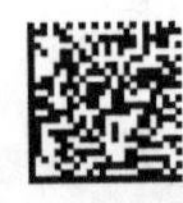